Firecrow

Mike O'Connor

First published in Great Britain, 2023.

Lyngham House, St Ervan,
Wadebridge, Cornwall, PL27 7RT

© Mike O'Connor, 2023

The right of Mike O'Connor to be identified as the author of this work has been asserted in accordance with the Copyright, Designs and Patents Act 1988.

All rights reserved. No part of this book may be reprinted or reproduced or utilized in any form, or by any electronic, mechanical, or other means now known or hereafter invented, including photocopying and recording, or in any information storage or retrieval system, without the permission in writing from the publisher.

British Library Cataloguing in Publication Data.
A catalogue record for this book is available from the British Library.

ISBN 978 0 954106 87 4 (paperback)
ISBN 978 0 954106 88 1 (eBook)

Cover illustration: collage by the author using a photo of a chough at Mizen Head, County Cork © 2007 by Keith Marshall of Whitstable, Kent.

Other graphic elements are by the author, by Susan Samm, or from www.clipartlibrary.com, www.rgbstock.com, or commons.wikimedia.org, and are used in accordance with their respective licenses.

FOREWORD

The arms of Cornwall are fifteen gold bezants, supported by a miner and a fisherman. The crest, standing above the symbols of the Duchy and its people, is a distinctive black bird with a red beak and legs. In its talons is a crown. The bird is a Cornish chough. This achievement of arms says much about Cornwall's heritage. In particular, the chough is a unique symbol of Cornish identity.

This book celebrates the chough and all it stands for. It is fiction, but much of it is realistic, and it is only right to declare certain fabrications.

There is no cottage on the headland beside Ponsontuel Creek; the location is private land.

Porthreun, which means Seal Cove, is an imaginary location between Black Head and Kennack Sands on the Lizard.

The dates of Lt. Col. Benjamin Hervey Ryves, distinguished founder of The Cornwall Bird-watching and Preservation Society, are 1876-1961. The tale implies they were rather later.

The true story of the chough's return is at the end of the book.

Also, although some estates in Falmouth had rough areas in the late 20th century, great steps have been taken in increasing civic pride and cohesion. There has been a huge reduction in petty crime and anti-social behaviour, even though the challenges of few job opportunities and expensive housing have not gone away.

Notwithstanding my anthropomorphism, choughs are wild birds and should be treated with respect. Disturbing them is illegal.

Finally, Fowey is pronounced Foy, and the dialect phrase 'mazed as a curly' means 'as confused as a curlew!'

ACKNOWLEDGEMENTS

I salute the many volunteers who helped the chough return to Cornwall and stay here: members and management of the National Trust, Natural England, the Royal Society for the Protection of Birds, the Cornwall Bird-Watching and Preservation Society, and many tenant farmers and private individuals.

I'm grateful to many story-telling friends for their support of my endeavours. I am especially grateful to Derek Reid for the tale of the White Spitfires, which he was given by a Mr Redmond in Cheshire in 1967.

CONTENTS

The Calling	1
Flight into the Unknown	2
The Storm	4
The Paintbrush of Resurrection	6
A Very Old Story	10
Freedom	15
A Disastrous Lack of Chocolate	17
We Have Made a Friend	20
Well Met by Moonlight	21
An Elegant Courtship	24
The Golden Bird of Day	26
Proper Cornish	31
The Vigil Begins	36
A Stratagem Worthy of Odysseus	42
Sky in the Morning	45
The Watchers of the West	49
Hot Cross Buns	53
Easter Eggs	55
The Pilgrimage	59
The Brothers	62
Home	64
Accused	66
The Three Skilful Brothers	73
Flora Day	76
Sky-Gazing	81
Seagull	84
The Three Fortunate Bequests	86
Four Legs Bad	90
A Riot in the Nursery	93
White Spitfires	94
Steps into the Unknown	97
Aerial Combat	100
Traffic and Pasties	104
Defying Gravity	105
Flying School	107
Born in Cornwall	109
Absent Without Leave	111
Two Barrels	114
Really a Family	119
Sixth Sense	121
The Return of the Native	123
When the Nightjar Calls	128

Firecrow	130
Mackerel Sky	133
Return to Clome Cottage	135
The Forever Nest	137
Chronology	139
Reference	140
The True Story	141
What to Do	142
The Cornwall Bird-watching and Preservation Society	143
The Royal Society for the Protection of Birds	143
Natural England	143
Corvids	144
The Royal Air Force on the Lizard	145
About the Author	146
Books by Mike O'Connor	147

East Kerrier

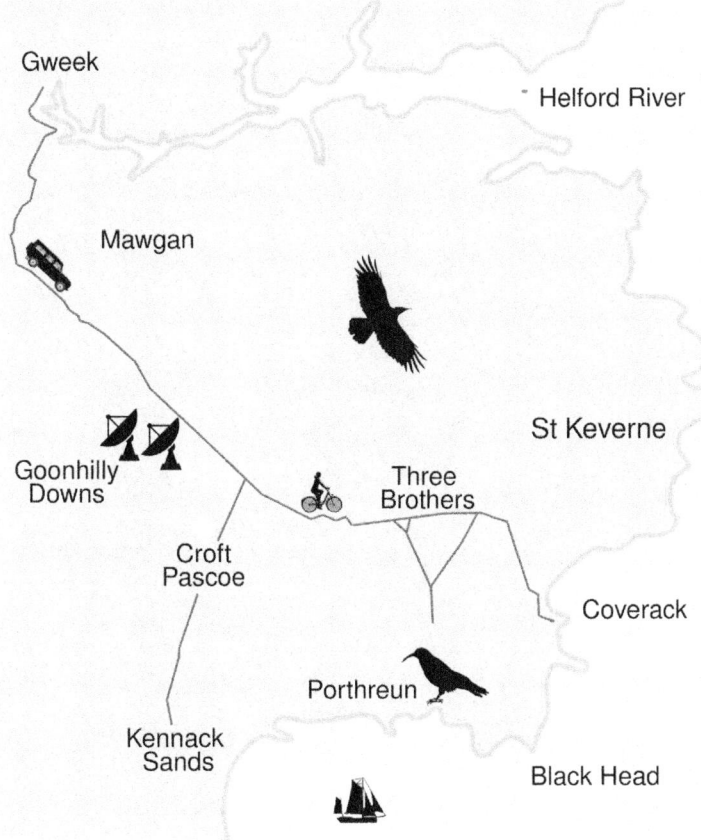

The Calling

At first it was almost imperceptible.

In the three years since he had left his parents' nest, he had not felt anything like it.

The young bird did not know if it was something heard, felt, smelled, or even tasted on the air. It did not come from the dunes behind him, or from the low cliffs on which he roosted with other adolescent birds. It did not come from the ancient sands or the waves which washed over them. It was not borne on the wind.

Yet it was present, day after day, and especially night after night.

It was soundless, but he simply identified it as 'the calling.'

He sensed it more and more with each passing sunset. He wondered if it was indeed growing stronger or if he was growing more sensitive to it. Whatever it was, although intangible it seemed to be very old. He sensed that it was something his ancestors once knew and were now trying to re-awaken. It was as if it were a fire slowly coming to life from and ancient grave of ash and embers.

"I heard it again last night."

"We heard nothing."

"A keening, a calling …"

"You must have been dreaming."

Next morning, they found he had gone.

Flight into the Unknown

The young bird woke in the middle of the night. He was immediately alert; there was no way he could have returned to sleep. The Moon-Bird was at its zenith and around it was a halo of coloured light – a circular moon-bow. It was so bright that it outshone the lighthouse, the Phare de l'Îsle Vierge. The bird rose and then perched on the edge of the nest, but for only a moment. With conviction he pushed forward, spread his great black wings, and silently rose into the night.

He was called by an instinct he could not resist. A long-forgotten memory embedded deep in his family unconscious had surfaced and told him this was what he should do. He was young but he was fit, and he obeyed the call with confidence, flying steadily and boldly into the darkness.

The wind was from the south-west and below him the endless ranks of waves approaching from the Atlantic appeared as alternating lines of light and shadow fleeing from the moon. Taller, breaking waves created a silver weft drawn across the great warp of the ocean. Behind him the lighthouse shone out, beckoning to him every five seconds; but try as it might, it could not call him back.

His feathers were as black as the night, but they shone in the moonlight, and with each beat of his wings, the colours of the moon-bow flickered across the gleaming span, as he powered into the darkness.

Soon the coast was far behind. Even the loom of the lighthouse was no longer visible, and he felt that special sense of alone-ness that sailors feel when out of sight of land. In those moments the sea, the night and the bird were as one. The steady rhythm of his motion was relaxed, assured; he felt he could fly for ever.

Far above him a shooting star streaked across the sky. Higher still the silver Star-Birds flew silently across the broad arc of the heavens. They were so high he could not hear the beating of their wings. Their course was almost at right angles to his own. Yet his sense of direction held him on course, an internal compass that let him understand the nightly flight of the stars. In the east they rose, in the west they set. It had always been that way. It would always be that way until the day when the Star-Birds were called from their resting place and returned to the land of their birth.

The Storm

After two hours of flight, the moon's light faded and disappeared. In the darkness, the approaching cloud was unseen. The bird's first perception was of sudden heavy rain. In such conditions he would normally have landed and sheltered, but there was no land in sight. Then it began to hail, and the creature sensed he was in a downdraft. In seconds he could hear the waves close beneath him; he was driven so low he could feel the salt spray. To stay above the waves, he beat his wings more rapidly. Suddenly he felt weary, but there was no option but to continue.

Then at once the hail ceased; the downdraft was gone. The black bird sensed the waves receding. He stopped beating his wings, but found he was still climbing. For a moment he relaxed, content to regain altitude and soar. But now he was at the centre of the storm, caught in a huge convective up-draft. Though he tried to dive he was carried higher and higher. Soon the air around him was freezing. He shook the icy rain from his wings, but even as he did so, he felt the coldness numb his body. The air was thin, he struggled to breathe. He could hardly move his wings; his mind too was numb; he had never known such cold.

The bird was almost unconscious when he felt his motion change. With each second, he felt marginally warmer, but he realised that again he was being driven down towards the sea. For a second time he struggled to remain above the waves.

Above him he saw the flash of lightning; it was frighteningly close. Peals of thunder tolled across the black ocean, echoing from wave to angry wave. The breakers roared endlessly and seemed to be getting closer and closer.

He had now been flying for three hours. He was bitterly cold and wearier than he had ever known. Once again icy rain and hail beat on his wings. Imperceptibly the beating of those wings slowed. Try as he might he could not maintain altitude. As his wings slowed so did his pulse, so did his mind. The once magnificent bird became a ragged bundle of flesh and feather, falling helplessly into the night.

The Paintbrush of Resurrection

It had been a wild night in west Cornwall. A great cumulonimbus cloud had passed just south of the Lizard peninsula. The cloud towered to a height of over thirty thousand feet, where it spread in a massive anvil-shaped head. Its powerful convective air currents brought strong winds, heavy rain, and hail. But by the dawn, driven by the prevailing wind, it had moved on up-channel, leaving Cornwall with clear skies. It was still chilly, but the sun was warm. Soon the tamarisk and thrift on the cliff edge, beaten down by the storm, were upright and turning to the sun.

Matthew and Josephine Williams had pedalled their bicycles from the village of Gweek to Porthreun, south of Coverack, to watch the seals. The name Porthreun means 'seal cove' in Cornish, and there was the hauling-out beach for a small colony. Inaccessible and far from most tourist haunts, it was known only to a handful of local people. Quietly the children lay on the cliff top, looking for any injured creatures, and counting the pups. In Gweek, close to where the children lived, was the National Seal Sanctuary founded by Ken and Mary Jones. Matty and Jo knew them well, and regularly reported on what they observed. Their counting task complete they tiptoed away from the cliff edge.

"Oh, no!" exclaimed Jo.

"What is it?"

"It's a poor dead bird, it must have been caught in the storm."

Matty reached down to touch the bird. In the morning sun its feathers, although black, somehow reflected all the colours of the rainbow.

As his fingers gently touched the wing it moved. The bird opened one eye.

"It's alive. Exhausted and half frozen, but it's alive. It needs warmth, drink, and food."

"What do we do?" asked Jo.

"I think we take it back to Aunt Jenny; she knows about these things. Get the sandwich box. We'll line it with our handkerchiefs and tissues. Use your pencil to poke some air holes in the lid. I'm sure it will feel safe and calm in the warm and dark."

Matty gently lifted the bird with two cupped hands, each covering a wing, and very carefully lowered it into the box, and replaced the lid. With elastic they attached the box to the rack over the back wheel of Jo's bike and pedalled the ten miles back to Gweek.

It was true. Jenny Powell was indeed a knowledgeable and capable woman. The District Nurse in a farming community by the sea, she was practical and sympathetic. She was the sort of aunt that children love to have, full of energy and bright ideas.

It was typical of Jenny that she had volunteered to look after her niece and nephew whilst their parents were overseas. Their father had a secondment teaching British nationals in Oman, accompanied by their mother. So, the children moved into Clome Cottage, and were sent to school in Helston.

"What have you got this time?" She asked as they pushed their bikes up the path to the cottage.

In the kitchen Jenny looked at the bird. It was awake, sitting in the box. Its eyes were sunken and dull, and the skin around them was wrinkled.

"It's weak, cold, and thirsty. What we must do is gently warm it and then give it a special drink."

Jenny tucked some old woollen socks around the bird and put it on a shelf above the kitchen range. Then into a cup she poured some lukewarm water from the kettle. To it she added a little sugar and a few grains of salt. Then she went to the drawing room, searched for a few minutes, before returning triumphantly with her paint box, from which she took a brush.

They were startled by a call from the shelf above the range, "Chee-ew-it, chee-ew-it."

"That is a good sign," said Jenny, gently placing the box on the kitchen table. She dipped the paint brush in the special drink and painted the fluid on the side of the bird's beak. It raised its head to swallow. In turn the children took the brush and continued feeding the bird. Soon its calls were more frequent. The bird was looking round about it and its jet-black eyes were now not so dull.

"What sort of bird is it?" asked Matty.

"I'm not sure," said Jenny, "It's certainly not a resident, or even a frequent visitor. But I have an idea. I must phone the colonel to find out."

"A colonel!" exclaimed Jo, "That sounds very grand."

"Not 'a' colonel, 'the' colonel! Lieutenant Colonel Benjamin Hervey Ryves of the Indian Army. He lives up at St Mawgan in Pydar. He knows more about birds in Cornwall than anyone else and he's an expert in one rather special species."

Jenny went into the hall where the phone sat on a table by the door. Ten minutes later she returned smiling from ear to ear.

"I was right," she beamed, "Our feathered friend is a chough. You can tell from the red beak and legs. They used to be common in Cornwall, but they died out here after the Second World War. Now they just live in Wales, Brittany, and Ireland."

"So perhaps ours came from Brittany," said Matty.

"And was caught in last night's storm." added Jo.

"Which is why it was so tired and cold," concluded Jenny.

There was a cry from the sandwich box to confirm the hypothesis.

The feeding continued all morning. After lunch there was a knock on the door. It was the bearded figure of Mr Boscregan from Ponsontuel Cottage.

"How were the seals?" he asked.

Mr Boscregan loved the seals and always asked about them.

"Very good," said Matty, "There were thirty-two on the beach: the beach master, sixteen females, eight pups, and seven adolescents."

"And no injuries from the storm," added Jo.

"That's good ... ," began Boscregan.

He was interrupted by a very loud 'Chee-ew-it.'

"My word! That sounded like a bird in the kitchen."

"It is!"

"It's in that box on the shelf. We rescued it."

"Colonel Ryves says it's a chough."

"Amazing, the king has returned!" said Boscregan.

"What do you mean?"

"Let's sit down and I'll tell you a story."

A Very Old Story

Sitting round the kitchen table they listened intently as Mr Boscregan began to speak.

I'm sure you've heard of King Arthur; he was born at Tintagel Castle, high on the cliffs of north Cornwall. Because Arthur was the son of Uther Pendragon, king of the Britons, he was the rightful heir to the throne. But Uther had many rivals who would want to do away with the new-born child. Uther's adviser, Merlin the magician, suggested it would be safest if Arthur was brought up in secret.

So, one dark night Merlin took baby Arthur, slipped out of the gate, through the shadows of Tintagel, and smuggled the child to Wales. There lived Sir Ector, the most trustworthy of knights. Sir Ector had agreed to become Arthur's foster father, and bring him up with his own son, Kay. So it was that Arthur was bought up as if he was Sir Ector's son. As he grew, in turn he learned the duties and skills of a page, a squire and a knight.

It was about fifteen years later that Britain was invaded by an army of Angles. Uther defeated at them the battle of St Albans. But he did not know that before they fled, the Angles had secretly poisoned the water. In the days after the victory feast, Uther and many of his men grew sick and died.

So, all the knights had to go to London to choose a new king. Sir Ector took Kay and Arthur with him. There, while the knights were all in church, a large block of stone appeared outside. Embedded in the stone was a sword. An inscription on the stone read: 'Whoever pulls the sword out of this stone is the rightful king of all England.'

All the knights wanted to pull the sword out, but try as they might, even the strongest failed. They didn't know that it was a magical stone made by Merlin, to make sure that the true heir became king. For over a year knights tried and tried to remove the sword. No one could do it.

At the end of the year a special tournament was held. Alas, when Sir Ector got there, he found that his sword had been left behind in his lodgings. Arthur was sent to fetch it.

Arthur searched high and low but could not find Ector's sword. He wondered how his master could take part in the tournament. Then he remembered the sword in the stone outside the church. Thinking nothing of it, he went to the church and pulled the sword out of the stone.

When Arthur returned with the sword, Sir Ector realised it was not his, so he asked Arthur where he had got it. Arthur explained that he had taken it from the stone outside the church. When all the knights realised what Arthur had done, they were amazed, and they made the 16-year-old boy King of England.

Arthur held his court at Camelot and ruled for many years. His Knights of the Round Table had many adventures. He fought twelve great battles and defeated the Saxons. He had a beautiful wife called Guinevere. But then the city of Rome, the centre of western civilisation, was sacked by the Goths, so Arthur set out to retake the city. He appointed his nephew Mordred to rule Britain and keep Guinevere safe while he was away.

But Mordred was treacherous. He locked up Guinevere, and when Arthur returned, he refused to give back the crown. So, instead of returning to a hero's welcome, Arthur had to fight Mordred and his men. The battle took place at Camlan, which some say is near Camelford in north Cornwall. The battle lasted all day, and the slaughter was great. As dusk was falling Arthur fought and killed Mordred, but was himself grievously wounded, some say mortally. Arthur was placed in a magic boat sailed by beautiful maidens, who tended his wounds as they sailed away from the shores of Cornwall. Now Arthur sleeps with his knights in a great hall underground, waiting for the day when his services will be needed to defend his people once again."

"Is that true?" asked Jo.

"It's just a story. But there's probably some historical truth in it, but just what and how much we will never know. It's often like that with stories. But the names are right. For example, near where the Colonel lives in St Mawgan you find farms called Tre-Artor: the home of Arthur, and Tre-Modret: the home of

Mordred. Oh, and there is also a Tre-Drustan: the home of Tristan.

"But for us the interesting bit is the sequel to the tale. Here in Cornwall, we have a special ending to the story. After the battle Arthur was given magic powers by Merlin. One of Arthur's powers is to be able to change his form into that of a Cornish chough, so he can return to Cornwall without being noticed, just to make sure his kinsmen are all right. The beak and the legs of the chough are blood-red because of the blood that Arthur spilled defending his kingdom. If his people are ever oppressed or enslaved, Arthur will return with the knights of the round table. For that reason, the Cornish coat of arms has a chough holding a crown perched on top of the shield. That's one reason why it was such a concern for Cornwall when the choughs began to die out in the 1940s. So, if the choughs return, it means that Arthur can once again watch over his kingdom as he wishes."

"How old is that story?" asked Jo.

"I bet someone just made it up," guessed Matty.

"Far from it. The events of the main story supposedly happened about one thousand four hundred years ago. They were written down eight hundred years ago. The special Cornish ending was mentioned in a novel called *Don Quixote* that was published in 1605, so it's at least four hundred years old. At first the bird in the story was called a raven, but in those days, people didn't really distinguish between different sorts of black birds. But we know the Cornish had their own word for chough long before the naturalists did, because in about 1700 a scholar named Lhuyd included it in a book about Celtic languages: 'palores', it means 'digger'.

There was a moment of silence as the listeners absorbed the tale and tried to grasp its antiquity.

Boscregan broke the silence. "So, what's your chough called? It must have a name."

Jenny's brow furrowed, "Should we name him at all? Doesn't giving him a name imply a sense of ownership? But we don't want to own him; we want him to be free."

"It's what's in the heart that is important," said Boscregan. "We will never know what this bird calls himself; but giving him a name is for us just a sign of recognition and affection."

"Then how about Arthur?" suggested Matty.

"That's good, but to me it's a bit presumptuous," replied Boscregan.

There was an animated conference. Storm-rider, storm-bird, … they all seemed a bit contrived.

Mr Boscregan added, "In heraldry choughs were called Beckets, and the Latin name is Pyrrhocorax pyrrhocorax."

"That's a mouthful," said Jo, "What does it mean?"

"Fire Crow, it's because of the red legs and beak."

"It's a good description," said Matty, "But it's not really a name."

"How about Odysseus? He was a great traveller, famous for stratagems."

"What are they?"

"Cunning plans."

"Odysseus doesn't sound very Cornish."

Jenny said: "I read that choughs were once called Killigrews."

"Who were they?"

"A piratical family from Falmouth."

"I'm not sure our chough is a pirate; he seems more of a gentleman."

Boscregan gently tugged at his beard in thought.

"The Welsh word for almost any sort of big, black bird is 'bran'. In mythology a great Welsh king was called Bran. How about that?"

There were nods of agreement round the table.

So 'Bran' it was.

Freedom

All that afternoon and evening they continued offering Bran his special drink every twenty minutes or so. Sometimes he would ignore it, sometimes he would come back for second helpings. Very gradually his eyes became bright, and he began to look around him, but he still showed no sign of wanting to leave his box. That night Jenny pulled the kitchen curtains and shutters, so it was completely dark inside.

The morning dawned clear and sunny.

Matty woke to hear Jenny saying, "My, what have we here!"

The twins threw on their clothes and hurried downstairs. Bran was standing up in his box looking around the kitchen.

Jenny left the kitchen curtains pulled but then wedged the back door open. The morning light was streaming in. With a loaded paintbrush Matty quietly approached Bran and again the bird drank from the brush. Knowingly, Bran looked at Matty and Jo.

"Chee-ew-it," he cried.

Then, with a movement both swift and graceful, he leapt from the box, spread his wings, and swooped out of the door into the sunlight.

Jo gasped in surprise, "Fabulous!"

Matty was more cautious, "Will he be all right?"

"I expect so," said Jenny, "At this time of the year there are lots of grubs and bugs for him to feed well."

Outside, the gleaming feathers stirred in the spring air. Bran's wings were again strong; his sight was keen; it was if he had been reborn. The great Sun-Bird was well advanced on its daily flight, and Bran flew to the south and east, as if to join him in the heavens.

A Disastrous Lack of Chocolate

"It's a disaster," cried Jo, struggling in through the back door of Clome Cottage with a full shopping basket.

"What is?" replied Jenny, unconvinced. "Has Cornwall come adrift and floated out into the Atlantic Ocean?"

"Worse than that! No chocolate!" cried Matty, "We got the rest of the shopping, but there was no chocolate at all in Gweek Stores. Mrs Old said there would be none until the van came from Helston."

"That is indeed a disaster," agreed Jenny, "But it's rather strange; there were lots of chocolate bars in the rack by the door on Saturday morning. I wonder where they went. Still, I dare say you may survive! What's your favourite sort of chocolate?"

"Easter eggs. The sort with chocolate buttons inside."

"Yes, they are nice. When I was a girl, we had to make our own Easter eggs."

"Did you make them out of chocolate?" asked Jo.

"Did they have chocolate buttons inside?" added Matty.

"No, it was not long after the war. Chocolate was rationed; so were lots of things in those days. So, our eggs were just hens' eggs. But we used to decorate them ourselves to make them special. Tell you what, it has just started to drizzle. It's miserable weather for going out. I'll show you how to do it."

They gathered around the kitchen table. On it Jenny put a glass bowl and three eggs. Then from the drawing room she fetched her paints, a selection of brushes and a roll of sticky tape. She stuck a small piece of tape on each end of one of the the eggs. Then she took a pin and carefully made a small hole at each end. At the fat end of the egg, she wiggled the pin a lot. Then she very gently pushed in a small knitting needle to make the hole bigger and then she removed the sticky tape. Finally, leaning over the bowl, she put her lips over the hole at the narrow end of the egg and started to blow. A mixture of yolk and white flowed out of the bottom of the egg into the bowl. Then the children did the same.

"Excellent," said Jenny, "Scrambled eggs for supper."

Then they carefully washed the empty shells in warm soapy water and gently dried them with a tea towel.

"Then you just draw on them or paint them," said Jenny, "Poster paints or oils are best. Then if you want to keep them for a while, when the paint is dry you can varnish them. But these watercolours are fine for muted colours."

They tentatively dabbed, stroked, and drew on the eggs. Matty painted a funny face; Jo painted a bright geometric pattern. The results were variable, but surprisingly effective, and it was all good fun. The minutes passed quickly and soon it was time for tea.

That evening the western sky was glowing.

"Red sky at night, shepherds' delight," said Jenny.

"What does that mean?" asked Matty.

"It means that next day the weather will be fine and the shepherds, who work out of doors, will be happy."

Jo chipped in gleefully, "I know what that is!"

"What is it?"

"I learned it at school. It's called an old wives' tale."

"Maybe," said Aunt Jenny, "But that implies it's probably wrong, but often old wives know what they are talking about!"

Matty looked unconvinced.

"If the sky is red at about sunset time, that tells you that the sky is clear several hundred miles away to the west. As the prevailing wind is from that direction, those clear skies will be with us in something over six hours time."

Matty smiled, "Yes, that's very logical."

"Hooray for the old wives!" exclaimed Jo.

We Have Made a Friend

Next morning the rain had indeed passed. The sky was clear, there was a lively breeze, and Jenny was hanging out the washing. The back door was wide open to let the fresh air in. In the kitchen Matty and Jo were eating cornflakes for breakfast.

Suddenly there was a shadow in the doorway.

"Chee-ew-it."

Bran swooped into the kitchen and landed on the table between the sugar bowl and the teapot. The children gasped with surprise.

The paintbrush was still on the shelf of the kitchen dresser. With a slow, steady movement of her arm, Jo reached out and took it. She dipped it in the jam-jar of spring flowers on the table and held it out. Bran hopped forward and drank from the brush.

Then, in a flash of movement, he was gone.

For a moment the children were speechless. Then Jo began to cry.

"That was so lovely," she said.

"I think we have made a friend."

Next morning, they left the door open again, but there was no sign of the black bird.

"He's probably made a nest out on the cliffs," said Jenny. "I think he just came back yesterday to say thank you."

Well Met by Moonlight

Corvids are the family of birds that includes crows, ravens, rooks, magpies, jackdaws, jays, and choughs. They are clever birds. Like all Corvids, Bran had a good memory. Consequently, he had intelligence; he could learn from experience. Admittedly the cardboard-box nest had been novel, but it was understandably a nest. The humans that fed him were unlike anything he had encountered before. But their gentle ways allayed his natural wariness of the unknown. As they fed him using the paint brush, he understood they were his family, just as his parents, in another nest far away, three years before. Repeated feeding led him to remember and trust these humans, to see them as sharers of his world.

But with each passing hour, as his strength returned, he sensed the freedom that lay beyond the curtained window of the cottage. He could hear the breeze in the trees beside the Helford River and birdsong on the wind. Then the door was opened wide, and the morning light streamed in. When Bran extended his wings, it was an instinctive action. Irresistibly drawn by the call of the day he swooped through the door and flew towards the light.

Below him stretched a magnificent green tapestry. First was the dark green of the woodland by the river and its many tributaries. But beautiful though it was, there was nowhere he could easily feed. Further south the chequerboard of farmers' fields was more encouraging. Some were, literally, grass green, others bright with the promise of early crops. Beyond, the uniform jade and fern colours of Goonhilly Downs did not attract him. But beyond them lay the cliffs and the sea. This was a world he remembered from his first days out of the egg. On the cliff edge he found his own scent. Fluttering from one feeding ground to another he saw a narrow crevice high in the rocks of the cliff. Too small for a gull, it was a perfect roost for a chough.

Set back in that fissure, Bran swiftly built a rather scrappy nest, just enough to give himself somewhere sheltered and dry to sleep. He did not return to it every night, sometimes trying other locations, but that cliff at Porthreun was his favourite.

Of course, Bran was not the only bird there. At the foot of the precipice were razorbills and cormorants. Kittiwakes, fulmars, and gulls occupied the middle cliff. Bran was largely indifferent to them all. He fed away from them, on the short turf inland from the cliff top, seeking out the ants and grubs that were his staple, a diet occasionally leavened with seeds or berries.

At Porthreun, when the prevailing south westerly wind reached the cliff, the air was physically forced upwards. In turn this made the air above rise. On the cliff edge, Bran had only to extend his wings to be lifted heavenwards. Then, with the advantage of height, he could glide in any direction, having expended no energy at all. He used this technique to move from one feeding ground to another.

One evening, when the great Sun-Bird was about to take its rest, and the sky was painted with vermillion and amber, Bran was again at the cliff top. He could see the broad sweep of the coastline curving towards the Lizard, silhouetted against the sky. The reflecting water was every shade from pewter to gold.

Medhel an gwyns, soft is the wind at sunset. The great golden Sun-Bird reached its nest and the light faded. Silently Bran wished it a good night's rest.

Other birds returned to their roosts, but Bran waited with patience. This was his favourite time. Gradually they became visible, the great flock of silver Star-Birds that forever flew across the night sky, faithfully escorting the great, white Moon-Bird. And there she was! Beautiful, calm, high above every storm. Yet, at the same time she was powerful, commanding the tides to follow her serene progress, from shore to boundless shore.

Far below Bran, small waves murmured a playful song as they danced around the boulders below the cliff. The dark blanket of the ocean became a shimmering mirror of the sky. This was indeed Bran's promised land. Then from the darkness he heard a call.

"Chee-ew-it."

It was another chough. Another soul that, like him, had somehow made an epic journey across the sea. A feathered creature that had shared his calling and his great journey. She was strong, though weary from her flight.

As she landed on the cliff-top a few yards from Bran, the moonlight gleamed on her glossy feathers. Every colour in the world shimmered on her outstretched wings.

"Chee-ew-it," he replied.

An Elegant Courtship

The courtship of birds usually only attracts human attention when it involves extravagant ritual or exotic displays of plumage. But all birds have their own, very meaningful, language of attention getting, gift-giving, ritual movement, song, and dance.

Swallows perched on a line will coyly shuffle towards each other with a neat sidestep, then fly a lightning-swift tail-chase to their next perch. Chaffinches dance in an ecstatic upward spiral of joy, a spinning kaleidoscope of feathers and high-pitched sound. Hawks twist and turn in an aerial ballet. Seagulls march and strut, their beaks pointed downward. Choughs dance a minuet.

The sun cast a warm light on the cliffs of Cornwall. Small clouds watched the waking land. To the gentle music of the breeze and small waves, Bran stretched out first his right wing, then his left, then both together. Then he bowed his head low, arching his back and fanning his tail high in the air. Then he danced first to the left and then to the right. Of all avian dances it was the most elegant. His ballroom floor was the close-cropped turf of the cliff-top. The backcloth was the sea and the sky.

At first his new friend feigned indifference. Bran patiently repeated his dance, and by the third repetition her eyes followed his every move. Then he pecked vigorously at the ground. He slowly walked forward, dropped a tasty grub at her feet, then stepped back. She looked left, she looked right, as if not wishing to seem impressed. Then she quickly picked up the grub and swallowed it. But then she looked away as if uninterested.

The third grub was consumed immediately. Then she looked at Bran, took a hop towards him, then sprang into the air. She flew eastwards, with Bran close behind. They flew together but not in formation, each in turn rising and falling, a few yards one way, then a few yards the other. All the time they made little confidential, chattering calls.

Eventually they landed side by side, back where they had started. Each gave the other small presents of food.

Below them, at the waters' edge the music of the waves reached a small crescendo. Above them the clouds rose in salute. The courtship was complete, and all was well with the world.

The Golden Bird of Day

Bran woke at dawn. It was time for the golden bird of day to fly. Bran imagined the gleaming wings spreading and lifting the great bird into the heavens. So high! So far! Above the clouds the golden Sun-Bird soared, impervious to cloud or storm, magnificent, radiant, bringing light and warmth to every nest in the land.

As the Sun-Bird climbed higher and higher, the warmth from the great fire basket on its back reached out to the waking world. Over the land the warm air began to rise. Above the waters' edge the circling birds simply flew over the land to climb, and over the sea to descend. It was an effortless process. There was no flapping of wings, just the subtle trembling of feathers in the invisible streams of the sky. There the soaring bird was stationary, serene in its heaven, while the troubled earth rotated beneath its outstretched wings.

That morning such a bird looking downwards would have seen two figures lying at the cliff edge, gazing down into Porthreun.

" … Thirty-four, thirty-five, thirty-six, thirty-seven."

Matty and Jo were again counting seals.

Jo whispered, "Three more than last week. Two extra females, two extra pups, and one less adolescent."

Matty wrote the figures in a small note-book. Then they silently crept away from the cliff edge. Suddenly there was a rush of wind, a swift shadow in the sky.

"Chee-ew-it."

"It's Bran, he's come back to see us."

"Perhaps this is where he has chosen to live."

"It's near where we found him."

"That's amazing."

"Chee-ew-it."

Bran perched on a rock about ten feet from the children. They stood perfectly still. The the chough spread its wings and made a short fluttering flight towards them. It landed just a yard away.

"He knows who we are," said Matty.

"That's wonderful."

"Chee-ew-it." This time the sound came from behind them.

It was another chough, and they ducked as it flew right over their heads to join Bran.

"He's got a friend!"

For a few moments both birds pecked at various ants and beetles. Then, without warning, they winged their way along the cliff edge to the far side of the cove, making little chattering cries as they did so.

The children watched as the birds made repeated journeys back and forth.

"Look," said Matty, "I think they're building a nest in that crevice; do you see? It's about six feet below the cliff top, just above the sloping grass ledge."

"I think Bran has more than a friend; I think he has a wife."

"When we give Mr Boscregan the seal numbers, we should tell him about this."

"He will be very pleased."

They crept from the cliff top and mounted their bicycles. Fifty minutes later they were descending the steep track that led from Gweek Drive down to Ponsontuel Cottage.

In the creek by the cottage, an old-fashioned, two-masted sailing boat was moored. It was Mr Boscregan's yawl, Can Reun – Seal Song. Appropriately enough, its owner was sitting on the seat outside the cottage playing his violin, at the same time watching a seal that was swimming close under the stern of his boat and listening to the music.

"Mr Boscregan, we have some news!"

"From your voices I can tell it's good news."

The seal raised its head from the water, attracted by the children's voices.

"Yes, it is good news. We went to count seals, same as normal, and we saw Bran again, and he has a friend, and it looks like they are building a nest."

"That is indeed good news. The last Cornish Chough I heard of died in about 1973, and the last choughs to bring up a family were long before that. But listen! This is important: we must keep this a secret. Too many bird watchers would disturb them and deter them from breeding, and there are even some nasty people that would come and steal the eggs once they are laid."

"That's terrible."

"Yes, it is. If egg collectors keep the numbers of a species very low, that increases the rarity and the value of the eggs. Any normal person can see that, as well as being illegal, it is a destructive and very selfish activity. But thinking of more cheerful things, what is Bran's partner to be called?"

"We hoped that you could suggest a name for us!"

"I see. Well in that case let's call her Branwen. In Welsh mythology Branwen was actually Bran's sister; but a pair of choughs called Bran and Branwen sticks in the mind and flows easily from the tongue."

So, Branwen it was.

At Porthreun the Coast Path turns north and cuts the corner on the landward side of the headland, where there is a prehistoric burial mound. To approach the cliffs on the east side of the porth, a rambler would have to leave the path, scramble across the ditch and bank that once defended the headland and push through a natural barrier of gorse and hawthorn. But, having persisted in this prickly and uncomfortable process, the explorer would been close to Bran and Branwen.

The flight paths of the choughs were unlike the others on the cliff. Avoiding the usual feeding grounds, they flew repeatedly between the cliff and the nearby clumps of thrift and fronds of tamarisk, compact bundles of colour and webs of graceful movement. The birds worked single-mindedly, only occasionally changing their routine to feed.

In its cleft in the rocks, the site was perfect: sheltered and safe. But what had been adequate as a casual roost for a single male, was quite inadequate for a family. Bran and Branwen rebuilt the nest. The outer structure was securely woven from dry twigs, roots, and plant stems, all padded with moss. Then they gave it a thick lining of wool, thistledown, feathers, and love.

After a day the nest was completely refurbished. It was snug and warm, perfect for the eggs that Branwen would soon lay.

Proper Cornish

Counting seals could sometimes be surprisingly difficult, with seals entering and leaving the water, or hiding behind rocks. But the following Saturday the seal count went well, and the twins were feeling very happy. To the east, out on the headland, Bran and Branwen swooped and played. In the crevice on the cliff their nest was invisible unless you had binoculars and knew just where to look. But as far as Jo and Matty could see the nest looked complete.

"I think Branwen will be laying her eggs any day now."

"I really hope no one disturbs her."

"On the cliff over there they are fairly safe. With all the furze and blackthorn between the Coast Path and the cliff edge, it's really hard to get at. Not much would disturb them accidentally."

"Repeated visits by holidaymakers might, especially if they brought dogs."

"It's a bit early in the year for that."

"The worst thing would be egg collectors."

"All we can do is try and keep the choughs and the nest a secret."

"So, leaving the bikes nearby would not be a good idea."

"Yes, and we should approach from different directions each time, to avoid making an obvious trail."

They left by the cliff edge by a roundabout route before heading back towards the lane end where they had left the bicycles. They were still west of Porthreun Farm when the quiet of the morning was broken by the incongruous sound of two-stroke petrol engines. They had hardly taken in the raucous noise when they had to jump out of the way to avoid being ridden down by three mopeds being driven at speed up the narrow path.

The riders were three boys a year or so older than Matty and Jo.

"Get out the way!" shouted the rider of the first moped as the twins flattened themselves into the furze bushes bordering the path.

The three riders stopped beside the Jo and Matty. They did not look happy. The leader shouted.

"I told you to get out of the way!"

"I'm sorry," said Jo, "We couldn't move any quicker."

Her apology was as instinctive as it was unnecessary; but, in any case, it was ignored.

"What are you doing here? Where are you from?"

Matty replied, "Gweek. How about you?

"No, you're not. You're never from Gweek, you're foreigners."

"We're staying with our aunt. She's the District Nurse ..."

"Oh, right, a do-gooder, living off poor people's taxes. And obviously you're incomers."

"... and our Mum comes from Truro."

"So, she married a foreigner. She's a traitor and you're a half-breed. I'm surprised we give you the time of day."

"So are we," countered Matty, his hackles rising.

"Quite the smartie pants aren't you. Look, for your own safety I'd stay away from here. It's not safe near the cliff edge. Unfortunate accidents happen to visitors."

Matty had taken a step back after the shock of this unprovoked hostility. Now he had gathered his thoughts.

"So where are you from then?"

"Falmouth, proper Cornish we are. This is our land. You're not welcome."

"I'd never have guessed," said Matty. Then he added, pointedly, "What's in your saddle bag?"

The question took the leader of the riders by surprise.

"Nothing that concerns you," he shouted angrily.

"Why are you so secretive?"

Now the leader was flustered.

"Look here nosey, it's us that asks questions here. We've met people like you before. Coming in big cars, blocking our lanes, using Cornwall as a playground."

"We came by train," said Jo.

"And bicycle," added Matty.

"Well, go back the same way and stay away. In particular, stay away from us. Crago, Billy Crago's the name. These here are Tonkin and Greaves. Remember the names. People avoid us, and if you're wise you will too. Enjoy your walk home."

The mopeds roared away down the path scattering stones and leaving tyre tracks. Small birds called out, taking to the air in alarm.

Deeply troubled, Matty and Jo returned to their bikes. All the people in the village were very friendly. They got on with the twins really well, and they loved and respected Jenny.

When they reached the bikes, Jo cried out, "I've got a flat tyre."

"So have I," grimaced Matty. He reached for his pump.

"Hey, I can't pump up my tyre, the valve's missing."

"Same here."

"Those boys must have taken them."

"I'm sure that's against the law."

"Yes, it's theft and criminal damage."

"We are going to have to walk home."

Disconsolately they started to push the bikes homeward.

"Those three boys, as well as being horrid, I'm sure they were up to no good. I think they could have been bird nesting. Crago's saddle bag had curious bulges that could have been made by egg boxes."

"What shall we do?"

"What can we do?"

It took them over four hours to push the bikes back to Clome Cottage. Jenny was in the kitchen, rather vexed.

"What time do you call this? You were supposed to be home for lunch, and now it's way past tea-time."

Matty, very weary, looked as though he might cry. Jo was flushed. Jenny immediately realised that something was terribly wrong.

"OK, you're not in trouble. Tell me what happened."

The children explained.

"Hmm. That is malicious, criminal. Actually, several local farmers have told me about three youths from Old Hill in Falmouth creating mayhem: trampling crops, leaving gates open, that sort of thing. I wonder if it's the same parcel of rogues."

"I think they may have been bird nesting as well," said Matty.

"That's illegal too," added Jenny.

" … and they weren't too far from where Bran and Branwen have their nest on the cliff," added Jo.

"That is a worry. But it's hard to know what to do. Anyway, supper is on the kitchen table. Sit yourselves down and tuck in."

Jenny went into the hall. From the kitchen the children overheard her using the telephone.

" … yes, Mrs Old, valves for bicycle tyres, they are needed as soon as possible."

The Vigil Begins

It was a bright new day. Breakfast was over and, as it was a Sunday, under clear skies Jenny herded the children to church. But despite resolutions never to bear a grudge, and the imprecation of the Lord's Prayer to 'forgive trespasses', the hurt was still there. Back at Clome Cottage Jo was vociferous.

"All the people here in Gweek are really friendly. When you pass someone in the lane, if you smile, they smile back. If you say good day, they reply in a friendly way. So why were those boys so horrid? We had done nothing to them."

Jenny replied, "They've heard others, I'm sure. I'm not defending them, there's no excuse for rudeness, let alone sabotaging your bikes, but we Cornish people do have reasons to complain.

"Cornwall was the first place the Industrial Revolution reached, back in the days when mines were prosperous. But it was also the first place the Industrial Revolution left, when the price of tin and copper fell, and mines closed. Unemployment in Camborne-Redruth is 27%, the highest in Britain. But redevelopment money doesn't come here. It goes to the north-east of England and South Wales where similar problems affect more people and get the attention of more politicians."

Jo was indignant, "Those boys were rude to complete strangers. It's not as if we're rich. Our grandparents live in a railwayman's cottage and a council house, but they are kind and polite. Dad's just a teacher, not a millionaire. We couldn't afford mopeds, even if we were old enough to ride them."

Jenny agreed, "Yes, you're right, xenophobia doesn't help. It just makes enemies when what we need are friends."

"What's xenophobia?" asked Jo.

"It's hating people just because they're foreigners. It's a long word for racism."

Matty, who had been listening carefully, shook his head. "I think they had something to hide. They shouldn't have been riding mopeds on the path, I'm sure it must be illegal. But it's not even a good place to ride. They were there for a reason. Their saddle bags were bulging; I bet they had just been pilfering or egg-collecting and they don't want us catching them at it in the future."

Jo continued, "Then what about Bran and Branwen? We can't hide them. Those boys will see them flying around."

Jenny suddenly became very business-like. "During the week, unless they play truant, those boys will be at school, like you. So, at weekends and holidays you or I will have to keep watch at Porthreun whenever we can, but without disturbing the choughs and without giving any indication where the nest is."

Matty looked thoughtful. "There must be something else can we do."

"We should be keeping watch right now," said Jenny. "Let's make a picnic, then I'll take us all to Porthreun in the Land-Rover. We can keep watch, eat the picnic, and tell stories till it's time to come home."

Before long Jenny's trusty Land-Rover was making its way towards Goonhilly Downs, and soon the great satellite dishes were in sight.

"There's King Arthur," said Jenny.

In response all eyes scanned the horizon for a medieval hero.

"Where?"

"There!"

"Where?"

"There! Arthur is the name of the biggest dish. It was named after King Arthur."

"Why?"

"It's a nickname, more fun than calling it dish number one."

"Do the others have names?" asked Matty.

"I don't know about all of them. The biggest is Merlin. The others include Guinevere, Tristan, and Isolde."

"What do they do?"

"They communicate with satellites and space probes. The first ever TV broadcasts via satellite were picked up there."

"I don't think they look very nice," said Jo.

"It's just what you're used to," said Jenny. "Every lane has telephone poles and wires; towns have street-lights; and most houses have TV aerials but, because they're used to them, no one complains.

The Goonhilly satellite station brings jobs and income here. There's been something on the downs since the Second World War. Then it was radar stations, looking for enemy aircraft. There were huge aerials where the satellite station is now, and more at Trelanvean, near where we turn right to go down to the cliffs. They used to guide fighters from Predannack airfield near Mullion. During the war it was all secret. The locals knew they were there of course, but no one knew what they did."

A little beyond the satellite station they passed the lonely crossroads at Traboe Cross. Then, after a succession of left and right curves, at Zoar they turned south into the narrow lanes leading towards Black Head. At Porthreun Farm they were greeted by the farmer and his family, who inevitably knew Jenny from her rôle as the District Nurse. They left the Land-Rover at the farm, then walked to the cove. On the opposite side of the cove from the nest they found a sheltered hollow, sunny but out of the wind, a fine place for a day's vigil. There they took turns at watching. At the same time, they told stories, jokes, and riddles. Jenny began.

Once there were three lads from Cadgwith. At the end of the summer, they went to the Harvest Fair in Helston. A fine fair it was and a fine fair it still is. I will take you there come September. These three lads, they loved every minute of it. Now normally folk from the Lizard will always make sure they are home before dark, but not these lads. When the business of the day was over the ale houses did a fine trade, to which our three heroes contributed nobly. There were musicians and dancing in the streets, and our three heroes danced till they could dance no more. There were traders and sellers of hot pies and pasties, and our heroes revitalised themselves with pasties as big as Jan Bedella's fiddle. But then it was time to go home.

Now, 'tis a fair old traipse from Helston to Cadgwith; 'bout twelve miles. Most people would go past Cury Cross Lanes, Penhale, and Mount Hermon. But it was a fine starry night, and so the lads decided to go round by Garras and up over Goonhilly. They could see the Great Bear and the Pole Star, the belt of Orion, and the big letter W of Cassiopeia. But in the very centre of the downs, as they made their way past the old burial mounds, just by the standing stone that locals call the Dry Tree, the mist came down. It was so thick you could nearly lean on it. As the lads felt their way along the track, they fancied they could see faint forms in the mist on either side. There were sprites and spriggans, ghosts and ghouls and goblins. Bats and owls flittered around their heads. In the distance they could hear someone laughing wildly. Shivers ran down their spines and all the hairs on the back of their necks stood on end.

Then they remembered that the downs are supposed to be haunted by the ghost of a highwayman that was hanged at a cross-ways in the middle of the moor. They always hanged criminals at cross-roads, so that the ghost wouldn't know which way to go and would stay there rather than haunt people's homes.

Now the lads were nearing Traboe Cross. Every time a nightjar called, or a fox barked, they nearly jumped out of their skins. But at the cross-roads there was no sign of the ghostly highwayman. Breathing a sigh of relief, they headed south. By now it was three o'clock in the morning, but they knew they had only four miles to go.

They had hardly walked another half-mile when just to the right of the track they saw an unearthly white glow. There was no habitation for miles. The only thing there was Croft Pascoe Pool. As they gazed at the pool, out of the darkness came a ghostly, gleaming lugger in full sail, it was sailing straight towards them.

In an instant they had in their minds a vision of every Cadgwith sailor that had every been lost at sea, calling out for the three lads to join them in their ghostly death-ship.

Straight away the lads started running. They had never run so fast in their lives. They ran past Bray's Cot; they ran past Cargey Gate, and they didn't feel safe till they reached Kuggar. They felt so tired, but they struggled on past Poltesco and Ruan Minor. As they reached Cadgwith the first light appeared in the eastern sky, and they swore that never again would they stay late at Helston Fair.

Laughing, the twins took out their Ordnance Survey map, and traced the route of the hapless Cadgwith lads.

All day Bran fluttered to and fro. Branwen seemed to be making final adjustments to the nest before settling down for the evening. Jenny had brought her big bird-book which had pictures of choughs, their nests, and eggs, and they read all they could about them. A handful of walkers passed by on the Coast Path, but none of them showed any sign of wanting to battle through the blackthorn and gorse onto the headland near the nest.

The picnic was eaten, and the stories continued until the sun was low in the western sky.

Then, under clear skies the Land-Rover trundled home. Over Croft Pascoe Pool a curlew swooped low, heading for its nest.

A Stratagem Worthy of Odysseus

Next day Jenny was out on her rounds and, as it was the Easter school holiday, Matty and Jo were left on their own. It was high water, and the sunlight danced on the river as they walked up the lane to the shop.

"Good morning, Mrs Old."

"Hello Jo, hello Matty. I've got some bicycle valves for you. They came in on the van this morning. What happened? Valves normally last for years."

The children explained.

"We met three boys on the Coast Path. They were very rude. We think they took our valves out of spite."

"We had to walk home."

"But that's miles!" Mrs Old looked unusually serious, "I don't suppose they was riding mopeds, was they?"

"Yes, noisy and smelly."

"I've seen 'em. They've been in here a few times. They usually buy just a packet of sweets between them. I've 'ad problems with my stocktaking ever since. They were rude to me too; they're not nice kids. They headed off on the Falmouth Road. Still, 'ere's your valves. Is there anything else?"

"Yes, do you have any varnish please?"

"Sorry dear, I can't help you. They'll 'ave some at the boatyard over the bridge, but only big tins. Would there be anything more?"

"Yes, half a dozen of your smallest eggs please, and it doesn't matter if they're old."

Mrs Old furrowed her brow, "People usually ask for the biggest and freshest, not the smallest and oldest. How about bantam eggs?" She took a carton off the shelf.

"These are the right size; please can we have the lightest coloured."

Mrs Old looked even more surprised. Rolling her eyes and laughing, she took down four boxes.

"Here, you sort out what you want! Just don't break 'em."

Jo selected six eggs, paid for them, and happily said goodbye.

Mrs Old watched the twins as they walked back down the lane to Clome Cottage. Every few yards they stopped to pick up twigs, leaves, and scrapings of moss which they put in a large paper bag.

"Mazed!" said Mrs Old, "Mazed as a curly!"

Later that morning Jo and Matty were back at Porthreun, on the headland on the opposite side of the porth to the choughs' nest. The children were crouched above a crevice at the top of the cliff. In the crevice Matty placed an object made of twigs and moss and lined with wool, built on a small piece of slate, and firmly attached with glue. It was a decoy nest. In it were the three most realistic of six bantam eggs they had painted, copying the picture in Jenny's bird book. Then they heaped earth, pebbles, and dead grass round the nest, making it harder to see, but not too hard. From above it looked completely realistic, though an expert might have noticed that the eggs were slightly large.

"I know what Mr Boscregan would say," said Jo.

"What?"

"A stratagem worthy of Odysseus!"

"Let's hope it doesn't rain. With a lot of water, the stratagem might dissolve," said Matty. "It was a shame we couldn't get any varnish."

Jo looked thoughtful.

"I don't suppose it matters. This crevice is quite sheltered. If it rains a lot, we can always repaint the eggs or replace them with the others we practiced on back at home."

With the decoy in position, they moved to the sheltered hollow to continue the day's vigil. In the porth, seals danced in the clear water. Out at sea, a basking shark made its stately progress down channel.

Sky in the Morning

"Red sky in the morning, shepherd's warning," said Jenny.

There was a pause while Jo swallowed a spoonful of cornflakes.

"Is that another old wives' tale that isn't?" she asked.

"Yes, it is!" Jenny laughed. "The idea is that around dawn the red sky is caused by low cloud in the east, part of a weather system that is going to bring rain. You had better take plastic macs with you today.

An hour later Jo and Matty were again hidden in the sheltered hollow. As well as binoculars and picnic they were equipped with folding stools to sit on, and a tarpaulin to shelter under if needed.

Looking across the porth with the binoculars they could see that Branwen was now practically all her time on the nest.

Every so often she would stand to make final adjustments to the nest's lining.

"I think she might be close to laying her eggs."

"It makes me feel very strongly that I want to protect them. It's as if we are all part of the same family."

"Yes, I feel the same. I'm sure that Jenny and Mr Boscregan feel that way too."

"It's a shame everyone doesn't feel that way."

At the end of the day the twins were relieved to find that their tyres were still fully inflated, and the ride home was uneventful. They looked hopefully but there was no ghost-ship on Croft Pascoe Pool, only a pair of lapwings. There was no ghostly highwayman at Traboe Cross, but a lone kestrel, hovering above the heath, watched as the twins pedalled into the distance.

That night Mr Boscregan and his wife Megan were invited to supper at Clome Cottage. Evenings with them were always fun. Mr Boscregan had an endless fund of folk tales; he called it his 'word hoard.' Megan always brought Welsh cakes and wonderful tales of her childhood in Wales and her lovely foster parents.

It was Mr Boscregan that had told them that the name Gweek came from 'gwig', a Cornish word for village. So after the last Welsh cake was eaten Matty questioned him.

"Mr Boscregan, on the way to Porthreun, we cross Goonhilly Downs. I know what hilly means but what does 'goon' mean?"

"Aha," Boscregan smiled, "Does it seem hilly to you?"

"Not really, it's a long climb to get up there, but then it's quite flat, not really hilly at all."

"Sorry Matty, I am teasing you a little bit. On the old maps it was called Goonhelly with an 'e'. That's because it was originally two Cornish words: 'goon' which means moorland, and 'helghi' which means hunting. So, centuries ago it was moorland used for hunting."

> "But there's at more than one story here. A couple of the uninhabited isles of Scilly are called Ganilly, Great Ganilly and Little Ganilly, practically the same word as Goonhilly. Long ago it was much bigger than it is today, and there lived the Lord of Ganilly.
>
> "But over the centuries the Isles of Scilly have been steadily flooded by the rising waters of the world. Local people say there is a whole land that is now under the waves. Their name for that land is Lethowsow: The Milky Ones. It's what fishermen called rocks such as the Seven Stones Reef, where the white water is endlessly breaking.

Lethowsow had 140 parishes with fine churches, woods and meadows, fertile fields all fringed with tamarisk. There was a watchtower at the western-most point. The chief town was called the City of Lions and there, long ago, lived a boy prince called Tristan. But day by day the sea grew bolder. Every month at spring tides the ocean spread its salty fingers over the fields: tentatively at first, but bolder with every full moon.

The first to notice was a man called Trevilian. He was alarmed by the daily advance of the sea, so he wisely sent his wife and family to safety in the hills of Cornwall. Then when the highest tide of the year came, when the full moon of the equinox shone on the first Autumnal gales, the waters rushed across the fields as never before. Trevilian leapt onto his horse – he had no time to saddle it – and rode bareback ahead of the flood. The waves were getting closer and closer, but he reached the high ground at Perranuthnoe, east of Penzance, just before they could engulf him. That is why the coat of arms of Trevelyan shows a horse without a saddle emerging from the sea.

The governor of Lethowsow was called Vyvyan. He too noticed the daily advance of the waves. He was better prepared and had a horse ready saddled in his stable. When the great inundation occurred, he too galloped ahead of the waves. But his steed did not have the stamina of Trevillian's horse. The sea grew closer and closer and looked sure to engulf him. The waters splashed around one, two, three of the horse's hooves. Then the horse gathered the last of its strength and made a great leap. It landed safely, and not far from here, at Trelowarren, the Vyvyan family built a new house. So that is why the Vyvyan shield is surmounted by a white horse, fully bridled, with one foot over the waves and three feet in the sea.

But with every moment that passed the water rose more swiftly. The Lord of Ganilly realised he could not ride the twenty-five miles to Sennen before the water covered the land. So, he made his way to the harbour of Nornour and sheltered there until the harbour itself was inundated. Then he set out in an old-fashioned boat. Its high bow and stern protected him from the heavy seas. Its strong hull was made of precious oak and its sail was of leather, so it could stand up to the violent winds. Its flat bottom let him sail across the shallow waters. He landed safely on the beach at Sennen, and on the slopes above the sand he built a chapel in thanks for his escape. It was called Chapel Idne, the narrow chapel. It is said that Sennen Cove was for years called Porth Gone Hollye: 'the port serving Ganilly'.

There must have been other survivors: those who ran to the hills we now see as islands, or those who escaped in other small boats. But because the tales tell of 'sole survivors' it's clear that many were lost, and the flooding of Lethowsow left a scar on the memory of the land.

Fishermen say that on still days and moonlit nights they can still see churches and houses under the water. The hill on which stood the city of Lions is the Seven Stones reef. Fishermen call it 'Tregva' or 'The Town'. There, in their nets they find domestic items and diamond-shaped panes set in lead, the remains of casement windows.

The Lord of Ganilly made his new court on the safe high ground of the Cornish mainland. The Cornish for 'high court' is Lys Ardh, and it's been called Lizard ever since. On quiet nights the Lord of Ganilly could still hear the bells of churches ringing beneath the waves. Where once were 140 parishes there are now 140 islands and 140 stories."

When all the tales were over Mr Boscregan gave his thanks and made his apologies. "I've a busy time ahead of me for the next couple of weeks. You may not see me around too much.

The Watchers of the West

Next morning, the twins rose early. As they left Gweek, morning mist still shrouded the river, but as the road climbed, Matty and Jo found themselves in bright sunshine. Below them the Helford and its tributaries were rivers of cloud etched into the countryside.

The children arrived at Porthreun by nine. As Matty was unfolding the camping stools he made an unexpected discovery. He quietly said to Jo, "There's something strange here. The grass is still flat. I'd have thought it would have sprung back up after we left yesterday."

"Perhaps cliff-top grass just behaves that way. Perhaps it's because it's in this hollow. Perhaps the wind or rain beat it down."

"I'm not sure."

The day passed quietly. There were few walkers on the Coast Path, and those with dogs had them on leads. Bran flew and fed himself and his wife. Branwen occasionally made adjustments to the nest.

The choughs were not the only birds nesting. Below them on the the cliff face, herring gulls were busy with their own nests. Once or twice, when their flight-paths crossed, Bran and Branwen found themselves hassled by bad-tempered gulls. The gulls were larger, faster, and potentially dangerous, but the manoeuvrable choughs easily dodged them.

At the end of the day, for a change the children walked East, returning to their bikes via the promontory of Black Head. On it they found a small hut with windows looking to seaward. The notice over the door read 'H.M. Coastguard.' The two coastguards were friendly, and when they saw the twins approaching, they beckoned them in. They seemed pleased to have company.

For a few moments the children stood quietly and watched as the watchers scanned the sea through binoculars, occasionally pausing to write in a log-book, recording ship movements and weather observations. A small radio crackled and hissed, monitoring messages from ship to shore, and listening to the emergency frequency: Channel 16.

When the coastguards' immediate tasks were complete there were introductions.

"We are Jo and Matty Williams. We are living with Jenny Powell in Gweek."

"But of course," was the reply. Everyone knew Jenny.

"I am Billy Johns, …"

"… and I am Ed Treleaven. We live in the Coastguard Cottages in Coverack."

Ed, the younger of the two, concluded, "We are the watchers of the west."

"We know one of those!" exclaimed Matty.

"Another coastguard?"

"No, he's a giant at Pentire Point near Padstow. It's a story. He's a giant that King Arthur asked to watch for invaders, and he's been there for hundreds of years."

"I know how he feels!" said old Billy, "We watch the shipping too, making sure all is well. We look out for ships in distress, oil spills, that sort of thing. On our radio we listen out for distress calls and relay messages from ships to Coastguard Headquarters in Falmouth. I'm sure your giant would appreciate a radio and a decent set of binoculars. Here, try these."

He handed the children his binoculars. They were very powerful, and the view was clear from Lizard Point to Dodman Head. Not only could they see everything approaching Falmouth Bay; they could read the the registration letters and numbers of fishing boats: PZ for Penzance, TO for Truro, FH for Falmouth, and FO for Fowey.

"I understand," announced Matty, "It's the first and last letters of the ports."

"Nearly," said Ed, "but not 'zacly. How do 'ee spell Penzance?"

Old Billy spoke, "There have been lookouts here for centuries. Three hundred years ago they were watching for Barbary Pirates who used to come raiding for slaves to take to North Africa. They would light a bonfire to warn of a raid.

"Two hundred years ago they were watching for Napoleon's ships; and signalling the information to Falmouth where the frigate squadron was based."

"Was that by bonfire too?" asked Jo.

"No, they had a great flagpole with a cross-yard that could be seen from miles away. From it they hung flags, pendants, and ball shapes. A ball above a flag meant an enemy frigate or frigates close to the land. Two balls over a flag meant a cruiser. Three balls over a flag meant a ship of the line."

"After the war with Napoleon ended in 1815, the lookout was used as a huers' hut."

The twins looked blank.

"Huers were lookouts for shoals of pilchard. Darn it, they must have been fit! When they spotted a shoal, they had to run to Coverack to alert the seine boats!

"In 1914, they were looking for German warships. This hut was built in 1915, and it's been used by the Coast Guard ever since."

Ed, the younger coastguard was equally friendly, "What are you doin' here? We've seen you quite a few times. Most people pass once on the Coast Path, and we don' see them again."

"We are bird-watching, and looking out for people who might disturb nesting birds or steal the eggs. Also, we count the seals in Porthreun so we can tell Mr Jones at the Seal Sanctuary."

"That's very good. We like people who do that sort of thing. If you ever want to shelter here, or pop in to eat your sandwiches, you're most welcome."

Young Ed grinned from ear to ear, "Now then, how do 'ee spell Fowey?"

Hot Cross Buns

Good Friday dawned clear. The day's watching was warm and uneventful. On the way home, as they freewheeled down Gweek Drive, they saw an old tin teapot hanging from a tree. This was Mr Boscregan's secret sign to say they were invited to Ponsontuel Cottage.

Outside the cottage Mr Boscregan and Jenny were already chatting. There was a bonfire, with logs and a bench round it. Out of the cottage came Megan, dressed in very old-fashioned clothes and carrying a large wicker basket covered with a cloth. To the children's surprise she danced round the fire and began to sing.

Good Friday's here, and the old woman runs,
With one a penny, two a penny, hot cross buns.

Hot cross buns! Hot cross buns!
One a penny, two a penny, hot cross buns!

If you have no daughters, give them to your sons.
One a penny, two a penny, hot cross buns!

"That's good," said Jo, "It means that the girls get the buns, and the boys don't!"

"That's not fair!" shouted Matty.

"It makes a change," said Jo, "It's usually the boys get all the treats, even though they don't deserve it."

"How do you know we don't deserve it?"

"Everyone knows that!" Jo began to chant.

What are little boys made of?
What are little boys made of?
Slugs and snails and puppy-dogs' tails.

That's what boys are made of.

What are little girls made of?
What are little girls made of?
Sugar and spice and all things nice.
That's what girls are made of.

Before the fight broke out Mr Boscregan discreetly placed himself between the twins.

"It does seem an arbitrary judgement," he said, "Not exactly merit-based. But it's the buns that are supposed to be cross and not the children. Now if you want your buns to be hot you've got some toasting to do."

The twins were issued with a toasting fork apiece, and Mr Boscregan hung a blackened old kettle from a metal tripod over the fire.

"For hot cross buns it is essential to have lots of fresh butter and mugs of tea."

He was right.

Easter Eggs

Next Sunday was Easter Day. The twins were discomfited as Jenny made them put on smart clothes and then herded them to church. The little building was packed. There were the handful of regular church goers, and a host of people that went to church three times a year. All were made equally welcome, and everyone thought the church was beautiful with little vases of daffodils on every window-sill.

Back at Clome Cottage the twins' reward was two Easter eggs for each child, one from Jenny and one from their Mum and Dad.

The joy of unfettered chocolate was momentarily dampened by the thought of the twins' parents, five thousand miles away. Matty looked very glum.

"Chin up! They'll be back for the Summer-holidays," said Jenny, giving both the twins a hug.

Then it was Jenny's turn to look tearful as the children solemnly presented her with an Easter egg with chocolate buttons inside.

"Thank you very much for looking after us," they said.

Jenny cleared a lump from her throat. "Thank you for being great kids. Tell you what, let's take our eggs to Porthreun and make a picnic of it."

In a short while they had packed the picnic and the Land-Rover was again crossing Goonhilly Downs.

"Before the aerials it must have been very lonely up here."

"Yes indeed. A wild place. In the old days most people wouldn't cross the moor at night. Do you remember, it's supposed to be haunted by the ghost of a highwayman? He was hanged at this crossroads we are just reaching. …"

Instinctively both children looked outside.

Alas, there was no ghost, no highwayman, and not even a decent gibbet. But not far from the road they did see a hawk, hovering over the heath, looking for small mammals.

"How about bats, like in the story?" asked Matty.

"It's rather exposed and windy for bats," said Jenny, "But you find horseshoe bats in the coppices and the woodland on the edge of the downs.

A quarter of an hour later Jo, Matty and Jenny were hidden in the sheltered hollow. Looking across the porth with the binoculars they saw that Branwen was now permanently settled on the real nest.

Bran fluttered back and forth with food for his wife.

"I'm sure she's laying her eggs," said Jo.

Matty knew not to argue. Girls knew about such things.

"What better day for laying eggs?" asked Jenny.

Matty was smiling, "These are real Easter eggs; Branwen's present to the world."

"And Bran's too," said Jenny, "It takes two to make eggs fertile."

"I wonder how many?" asked Matty,

"My book says three to five eggs."

They all felt happy the eggs were laid, but also concerned for their safety. But there was no sign of the boys from Falmouth, and at the end of the day they happily motored home.

Descending Gweek Drive, they saw the tea-pot hanging from its tree, so they turned down the steep track to Ponsontuel Cottage.

"Happy Easter," cried Mr Boscregan, "Megan has made a special cake and wants us all to try it."

An offer of cake could not be refused. Soon they were sitting around the table. Tea and lemonade were duly produced. Then, rather coyly Megan brought in the cake. It was magnificent – a fruit cake with a thick layer of marzipan on top, and on that stood eleven marzipan eggs.

"It's called a Simnel Cake," said Megan, "My step Mum taught me how to make it. It was traditional to make one every Easter.

"Why are there eleven eggs on top?" asked Matty.

"I expect that's how many would fit," guessed Jo.

"Not at all," said Megan, "It's one egg for each of Jesus' disciples."

"But there were twelve of them."

"Ah yes, but Judas doesn't get one because he betrayed Jesus."

"That seems unkind, Jesus said we have to forgive people."

"That's true, but just because you forgive someone it doesn't mean there aren't consequences."

"What I think," said Mr Boscregan, "is that Judas could not forgive himself, and that's true for many of us who have made mistakes, big or small."

The idea of grown-ups making mistakes had not really occurred to Jo, and she seemed thoughtful.

The thinking was disrupted by Mr Boscregan.

"While you were out today, I remembered another mention of a chough, and I think it must be the oldest in the world."

Matty looked hard at Mr Boscregan. He didn't look *that* old.

"These words are about 2,750 years old. They're in Homer's 'Odyssey', the story about the warrior Odysseus, the one who was good at stratagems. On his way home from the Trojan war, Odysseus managed to upset the sea god Poseidon. So instead of taking ten days, his journey took ten years, and he had all sorts of adventures on the way."

"Once he was shipwrecked on an island belonging to a beautiful nymph called Calypso. Homer described it something like this:

> Many years ago, after the Titans lost their ancient war with the Gods, Atlas was made to hold up the sky forever. His beautiful daughter was exiled to an island at the very centre of the sea. Her name was Calypso.
>
> She lived in a beautiful cave. Around it was a wood, with alder, poplar, and sweet-smelling cypress, where birds long of wing would nest: owls and falcons and sea-crows with chattering tongues. There was a vine, rich with grapes. There were fountains, soft meadows of violets and parsley. It was a land of delights.

"I'm sure the 'sea-crows with chattering tongues' must have been what we call choughs. 'Chattering' describes exactly the sounds of choughs talking to each other. That Homer calls them 'sea-crows' implies they live by the sea. So, Bran's ancient relatives were nesting on the cliffs above Homer's 'wine-dark sea' a hundred generations ago."

The Pilgrimage

Easter Monday dawned clear. It was the last day of the school holiday. Jenny could not be persuaded into another day on the cliff-top, so Jo and Matty pedalled off on the familiar route towards Porthreun.

Their journey began at sea level. Then their muscles were very aware of the long climb out of the wooded valley of the Helford River on the winding lane called Gweek Drive; once the carriage road to the Vyvyan family's mansion of Trelowarren. After two miles, they passed the hamlet of Garras, the children took the road across the open heathland of Goonhilly Downs, where the great dishes of the satellite station gazed silently at the sky.

This was the highest part of the journey, about 340 feet above sea level. Mr Boscregan had explained that the heath was very special, unique.

"Watch out for the orchids!" he said.

This command gave the twins an unusual challenge. Matty and Jo had never actually seen an orchid and had no idea of its size. Matty had a vision of a giant plant, more like predatory rhododendron. When, eventually, it was found to be about ten inches tall, he was very disappointed.

On Crousa Downs, the twins turned right just by the ancient stones of the Three Brothers of Grugwith. Then came another two miles of gentle descent on narrow lanes fringed with bright clouds of hawthorn blossom. The lanes became tracks and ended in dense woodland. The bikes could be taken a little further, but the last yards were on foot to the cliff top at about 160 feet above sea level. It was a journey of nine miles that always took a little over an hour. Most of the lanes were sheltered with hedges of gorse, holm-oak, and blackthorn but a headwind on the open heath could easily add fifteen minutes to the ride.

It was a journey of contrasts, the deep wooded valleys of the Helford and its tributaries, the open heathland of the downs, the pockets of woodland, and finally the open cliff top.

Also, being the west of Cornwall, where the Cornish language was spoken well into the 19th century, the name of every feature of the landscape, every farm, even every field, was Cornish. The names often told of the history, mythology, and the people of that ancient land. With the help of a friend like Mr Boscregan, who knew Cornish language, history and folktales, the landscape came alive.

An advantage of the route was that when returning, tired and hungry at the end of the day, the last half of the journey was downhill, and they could free-wheel the last two miles down Gweek Drive.

It was not impossible for most of the journey to be in cloud. Tendrils of mist would swirl about the tops of the trees lining Gweek Drive. On such days, with most visual cues removed, the downs acquired a timeless quality. The white, wild Goonhilly ponies would move, wraith-like, on the periphery of the cyclists' vision. It was as if they were the ghosts of their ancestors that worked underground in the Cornish mines.

On one memorable evening the twins were later than usual returning to Gweek. It was misty, and in the dusk Croft Pascoe pool was illuminated with a strange flickering light.

"What's that?"

"I don't know."

"Let's take a look."

"It's rather eerie."

"That's where the ghostly lugger is supposed to sail."

Warily the twins crept to the edge of the pool. Alas, there was no ghostly craft sailing through the reeds. But Will o' the Wisp flickered magically around the waters' edge, dancing across the rushes, and mirrored in the still water.

Somewhere an owl called.

The Brothers

Outside Clome Cottage, the colours of the sunset played on the waters of the Helford River. Downstream a lone heron was silhouetted near Ponsontuel Point.

In her cottage Jenny lit candles. "They are so much friendlier than electric lights," she said.

The friends had just finished their supper and were chatting round the dining room table.

"Mr Boscregan," asked Jo, "On the way to Porthreun, past Goonhilly, on Crousa Downs there is something that the map calls a dolmen. It has a name: 'The Three Brothers of Grugwith'. But we went and looked at it on the way home. It's just three very big rocks. What is it?"

"That's a tricky question," Boscregan teased the end of his beard.

"Let's start at the beginning," he said. "Those are all old names, recorded for 250 years.

"I'll start with Crousa Downs. 'Crousa' possibly comes from two Cornish words: 'krows' and 'gwragh'. 'Krows' means cross, and as there's no wayside stone cross there, it probably just meant the crossroads. 'Gwragh' means old woman or witch. In Cornwall ladies called 'witches' were often the village wise-woman. So perhaps a wise woman lived at the crossroads."

"That's a lot to discover from one place-name," said Jo.

"It's surprising how often such deductions are right. Anyway, a dolmen is a prehistoric tomb. It has huge stone slabs for walls and another for a roof. It was once covered in earth and grass, but often the soil has worn away leaving just the stones, and in this case the stones have probably fallen down. The name comes from the Cornish words: 'tol' and 'men'. 'Tol' means hole or burrow, and 'men' means stones.

"Grugwith is also two Cornish words: 'krug' means a burial mound; 'gwydh' means trees. Perhaps it was a special place, groves of trees are associated with pre-Christian religion. You can tell that the name came from oral tradition because it gets spelled different ways. Sometimes it's recorded as Crugwith or Crugith.

"As for the 'three brothers', they are the three big stones lying flat that you have seen. They would only have become visible thousands of years after the tomb was made, when the surrounding earth was eroded. So, the people giving that name would have had no knowledge of the original occupants of the tomb, but they probably knew or invented a story about three brothers. As they were apparently buried or turned to stone together, then maybe the brothers were friends rather than rivals.

"So, now we must find the story! It has three friendly brothers, and we if can manage it, a sacred grove, a wise woman, and cross-roads! Many folk tales involve three brothers. You'd better start reading your Aunt Jenny's collections of folk tales to see if one fits. Tell you what, why don't you all come round for supper next Saturday. Megan and I would love to return your hospitality, and we can swap stories."

Home

The following Saturday the twins confirmed that Branwen was spending all her time on the nest. Bran worked steadily, ensuring his wife was well-fed.

"That's what boys have to do!" proclaimed Jo.

Matty looked thoughtful but carefully said nothing.

The children watched happily, at the same time reading, sketching, chatting, or arguing, in no particular sequence. In the middle of the day, they religiously counted the seals for the benefit of the Seal Sanctuary. Passing ships were always interesting. Small fishing boats scurried back and forth, and large tankers and bulk-carriers passed surprisingly close inshore as they headed into the anchorage of Falmouth Bay. The sea itself was a constant source of fascination, as was the sky.

Matty lay on the cliff-top gazing upwards. For some azure is defined as the colour of the sky on a clear day, but in truth there are not enough words in the English language to describe what he saw: the subtle gradations of colour, saturation, and intensity drawn across the heavens' arc. Vertically above him the blue was at its deepest. The colour faded towards the surrounding horizon, from rich cobalt, via indigo, sapphire, and azure, to a distant cyan. But onto that symmetrical palette the sun superimposed its own blinding brilliance, bleaching the colours of the sky in its wake.

Each hour saw change in the sky's spectrum of colour. Also on that day, which had begun cloudless and still, by mid-morning numbers of small, fluffy clouds appeared spontaneously over the mainland of Cornwall.

Half a mile inland from Porthreun the sun warmed the dark loam of a ploughed field. Then the earth warmed the air above it, only a fraction of a degree, but just enough to make begin to rise.

As it rose its place was taken by cool air from the surrounding fields, which was warmed and rose in turn. Soon, over the warm furrows, an invisible column of rising air reached to the heavens, arcing gently downwind as it did so.

Above the furrows the circling birds were sensitive to the minute changes in temperature and atmospheric pressure, and they could detect when the invisible hands of the rising air were lifting them. Spiralling far above the ground they maintained altitude with consummate ease and the sun warmed their feathers. Highest was the buzzard watching for small mammals. Below him smaller birds pursued insects. Others courted each other, calling and playing in the sun. But there were some that circled in the heavens for no apparent reason other than the sheer ecstasy of flight.

On the cliff edge Bran and Branwen would only rarely employ this mode of flight. They usually flew in the turbulent air close to the ground, near their source of food. Their flight was reactive, constantly responding to the up-drafts and vortices at the cliff-edge, and the gusts and eddies caused by trees, bushes, and outcrops of rock. The manoeuvrability and speed of reaction of the choughs was unequalled. They were fast, though not the fastest, but their aerobatic ability was peerless, and they loved the rough and tumble of the Cornish cliffs.

Jo and Matty could sense that, though the birds had come from far away, Cornwall was their natural home. It was something they understood, and they felt a great contentment.

Accused

The twins spent the following day at Porthreun, as usual watching the nest at a distance. Mr Boscregan had loaned them some high-powered binoculars that he used on his boat, so they could see very clearly from the opposite side of the porth. Most of the time Branwen was on the nest. Bran flitted to and fro, sometimes feeding himself, sometimes bringing food for Branwen.

"She's definitely incubating her eggs now." Jo still felt maternal.

"How long does it take for them to hatch?"

"Jenny's book says nearly three weeks."

"So, the chicks are due in the first week of May."

"It should be warmer by then."

It was mid-afternoon when Branwen stood, then flew to the clifftop and foraged for a few seconds. Jo was watching through the binoculars.

"Three," she cried, "I'm sure there are three eggs."

Moments later Branwen returned to the nest. They watched for another forty minutes, then it was time to return to Clome Cottage for tea, delighted to confirm that the eggs were laid.

Jenny was pleased too. "In that case," she said, "It's time for a special tea!"

There were sandwiches followed by celebratory scones with strawberry jam and clotted cream heaped on top. Jenny called them 'volcanoes.'

"The jam is the fire, and the clotted cream is all the smoke rising up," she said.

The twins were unconvinced about the vulcanism, but the scones tasted very good.

Then from the larder Jenny produced a magnificent cake covered in white icing. Drawn in food-colouring on the icing were two small black birds with red beaks and legs. Three small chocolate eggs were newly perched between them.

"It's a birthday cake," exclaimed Matty.

"I'm not sure if a baby chough's birthday is when its egg is laid, when it's sighted, or when it hatches. But eggs don't always hatch. Let's just call it an egg-day cake."

The egg-day cake was helped down with scoops of ice cream. Finally, all was washed down with cups of tea. It had been a magnificent meal.

It was about an hour later, when the dishes had been washed and dried, that the doorbell rang.

Jenny answered the door. Standing in the doorway, Sergeant Boxall from Helston police station was an imposing figure. With his helmet he was well over seven feet tall. Behind him were Crago, Tonkin and Greaves.

"I'm sorry to trouble you Miss Powell," said the Sergeant, "Please can we come in? I'd like to speak to Matty and Jo if you will permit me. I take it that in the absence of their parents you are acting as their responsible adult?"

"I certainly am," said Jenny, suddenly sounding much more like a district nurse and rather less like a friendly aunt.

She showed them in, and they all sat around the kitchen table.

"I'm sorry to tell you, Miss Powell, that I've just had a serious complaint about your niece and nephew. The Protection of Birds Act of 1954 makes it illegal to take the eggs of wild birds. As you may know the chough died out in Cornwall some years ago. I have been told that your niece and nephew have been seen stealing the eggs of the first pair to have laid eggs here since not long after the war. This is a very serious matter."

Matty blushed with indignation and started to speak.

"But we just …"

"Shh," said Jo.

"He's blushing because he's guilty." It was Crago that spoke.

"Yeah, proves it," said Greaves.

"Be quiet," said the sergeant, sternly. "You speak when I tell you. Matty, I'd like to look in the saddle bag of your bicycle if you don't mind."

"Sure," said Matty, quite unconcerned.

They walked outside to where the bikes had been left in the garden. Sergeant Boxall opened the saddle bag. In it were three light brown, speckled eggs.

"How do you explain these then?" asked the sergeant.

Matty was lost for words.

They went back inside. As it was a warm evening, they left the door open. Sergeant Boxall placed the eggs on the table. All eyes were on them.

Matty was close to tears.

"I don't know how they got there," he said, as tears started to run down his cheeks."

"Oh yes you do," said Crago.

"Excuse me," said Jo, "I need a glass of water."

"You'll need more than that," said Tonkin.

Seconds later Jo returned with the tumbler of water. Sergeant Boxall had taken out his notebook and was writing in it.

Before anyone could stop her, Jo grabbed one of the eggs and dropped it into the glass of water.

"Hey, what did you do that for …"

All conversation stopped. The egg did not sink at all. It floated right on top of the water. Where the water touched the shell, the markings slowly began to dissolve.

Jo spoke with surprising confidence, "These are not chough's eggs, they are bantam's eggs painted to look like chough's eggs."

Tonkin and Greaves looked taken aback.

Sergeant Boxall looked at Crago.

"Yeah, that's right," said Crago, "We wanted to protect the choughs, so we made a dummy nest. We painted the eggs and put them in it. We knew that these foreigners would fall for it. They don't understand country ways."

Jo reached to the dresser. On the shelf was the egg box. From it she took the remaining three eggs.

"Then how do you explain these?" she said. There was a hard edge to her voice.

"Yeah," said Crago, "They were the first three you took and brought back 'ere."

Now Jenny looked very angry. "Here is my paint box, here are my brushes, here is my bird book with the picture of the egg that Jo and Matty copied."

"That's right," said Crago, unabashed, "It's just like my paint set at home, and the book I got from the library."

Matty, his composure regained, held up a brush. "This is the brush I used. On the stem there are traces of the brown paint of the speckles."

"Whenever you use paints, that's bound to happen."

"We bought those bantam eggs at Gweek Stores eleven days ago. Mrs Old can confirm that," said Jo.

"It's clear to me," said Jenny, "That these three lads are making it up as they go along. They were taken in by the decoy eggs made by Matty and Jo, probably when engaged in illegal bird-nesting themselves. They planted the eggs in Matty's saddle bag; and then they made a false accusation against my niece and nephew.

"Sergeant, I would like to make a formal complaint about them. I suggest that you fetch their parents."

Sergeant Boxall looked confused. This was much more difficult that he had anticipated.

"Well, I don't know," he said, "It seems to me that either side could be telling the truth."

At that moment there was a flash of shadow in the open door. Matty was still holding the paint brush. Bran landed beside him, leaned forward, and drank from the brush.

"Chee-ew-it."

The bird drank once more, strutted majestically across the table, and swooped out into the garden.

"Sergeant Boxall," said Jenny, "My niece and nephew secretly rescued and nurtured the first chough to have landed in Cornwall for decades. That's why this bird trusts them. They have been protecting it, its mate, and their nest ever since. Do you think they would then steal the eggs? That is utterly illogical. I think you should look elsewhere for nest robbers, and the first place you should look is at these three rascals sitting beside you. I'm willing to bet that if you went to home of young Mr Crago here, you would find no brushes, no paints, and no library book, but you would find a lot of bird's eggs."

Crago looked horrified.

"It was Tonkins' idea, of course, …"

"No, it wasn't," said Jenny, her eyes blazing, "The others just follow you."

"… and Greaves had the paint set."

"The paints don't exist," asserted Jenny.

"Miss Powell," said the sergeant, "I'm afraid my radio doesn't work down in the valley here. Can I please use your phone. I need my colleagues to speak to the parents of these three boys. I suspect they may be in a lot of trouble. Making a false allegation is a common law offence, it's attempting to pervert the course of justice. Also, today these lads have been wasting police time, which is an offence under the Criminal Law Act 1967."

As the sergeant made his phone call Crago spat across the table, "I'll get you two for this! Nobody messes with me."

Then the three boys ran through the back door and headed up the lane. There was the sound of moped engines being revved up.

"They're getting away," cried Matty.

"They can run as much as they like," said Sergeant Boxall, quite relaxed. It won't help them a bit. Chasing them now is a waste of time and might be dangerous; they might fall off their bikes and get hurt. But those putt-putts will only do thirty miles an hour, and anyway they've got nowhere to go. They undoubtedly will be caught, and sooner rather than later. But now, Jo and Matty, I'm very sorry for all you have been through today. But thank you for answering my questions so clearly and I'm sure, so honestly."

"Sergeant Boxall," added Jenny, still looking very determined, "In my rounds as the district nurse, I have gathered a list of farmers between Gweek and Falmouth, all with complaints about gates being left open, livestock being disturbed, and crops trampled. You should speak to them. Also, you need to ask Mrs Old in Gweek Stores about chocolate bars that have gone missing. And as I understand you must be sixteen years old to ride a moped, you might want to check the exact ages of your three would-be witnesses, and also see if they have any insurance."

The sergeant went outside, scribbling frantically in his notebook.

Inside, Jenny, Matty and Jo had the biggest hug imaginable. They were laughing and crying at the same time.

"Bran knew. He knew we were his friends, and he came to help us."

"That was amazing," said Jenny, "It's time for second helpings of ice cream."

The Three Skilful Brothers

Ponsontuel Cottage was tiny. The kitchen table was not really big enough for four people, let alone five. The old expression for 'close together is 'cheek by jowl'. On this occasion the diners were definitely 'elbow by elbow' which was quite fun for a few minutes, but quickly grew to be rather irksome.

Mr Boscregan had found an ancient bottle of wine.

'A very fine vintage,' he exclaimed.

Jenny said, "In France the children drink watered-down wine, would you like to try some?"

Matty and Jo nodded, wishing to be both polite and grown-up, but secretly apprehensive.

Alas! It tasted horrible to adults and children alike, so everyone drank water instead. The twins gave a collective sigh of relief. But it didn't stop supper from being a very good-natured gathering.

"How did you get on with your search for the three brothers?" asked Boscregan, unabashed at his social setback.

"We found a story," the children chorused.

"Excellent," said Boscregan, "You've done better than me. I went to Helston library and found this old book: *The Illustrated Itinerary of Cornwall*' written by a man called Cyrus Redding in 1842. What he wrote was this."

> One day St Just came from West Penwith and paid a visit to St Keverne on the Lizard. The visit was very cordial, but after Just had left, Keverne found that some of his valuable church plate – gold and silver chalices and the like – had gone missing. The thief could only have been St Just! Keverne chased after him, but Just was too far ahead to catch up. So Keverne picked up three big stones and

threw them at St Just. They missed and landed on Goonhilly Downs. Those three stones are what we now call the Three Brothers of Grugwith.

"But Mr Redding doesn't explain how or why the stones got their name, so for me that's rather unhelpful and not very convincing. So please, tell me your story."

Matty looked at Jo. "We found this one in Grimm's Fairy Tales. Who's going to do it, will you?"

So, Jo began.

> There was once an old man who had three sons. Each of the sons wanted to inherit the house after his father's death; but their father loved them each the same amount and did not know what to do. But eventually he devised a plan. He said to his sons, "Go into the world and learn a trade. When you return, the one who is the most skilful shall inherit the house."
>
> The eldest decided to learn to be a blacksmith, the second a barber, and the third a fencing-master. They agreed a time when they would all meet at home again, and then each went on his way.
>
> They all went and found excellent teachers who taught them their trades well. The blacksmith shoed the King's horses. The barber only shaved dukes and earls. The fencing-master duelled with the best in the land. Each thought he was bound to inherit the house.
>
> On the agreed day the brothers came home. As, they were discussing how to show their skills a hare came running across the field. Straight away the barber took his basin and soap and whipped up a lather. As the hare came past, he soaped and shaved off the hare's whiskers whilst he was running at full speed, and did not even cut the hare's skin or injure a hair on his body.
>
> "Well done!" said the old man. "That was very good."
>
> Then up came a nobleman in his coach, rushing along at full speed. The blacksmith ran beside the coach, took all four shoes off

the feet of one of the horses and put on four new shoes whilst it was still galloping along.

"That was brilliant," said his father.

"Then it began to rain. The third son drew his sword and flourished above his head so fast that not a drop fell upon him. Then it rained still harder and harder, till it came down in torrents; but the son just moved his sword faster and faster and stayed as dry as if he were indoors. When his father saw this, he was amazed and said, "You are the master, the house is yours!"

The brothers didn't argue and, as they all loved one another very much, they all lived together in the house following their trades, and as they were so skilled, they earned lots of money. They lived together happily until they grew old; and at last, when one of them died, the two others grieved so sorely that they died too. Then because they had loved one another so much, they were all laid in the same grave.

The adults applauded the young storyteller mightily. "Well done," they cried, and Jo smiled and looked embarrassed at the same time.

"So," said Mr Boscregan, "The three Brothers of Grugwith were also buried side by side in the same grave. Do we think that could be their story?"

Flora Day

Neither Matty nor Jo felt at home dressed from top to toe in white, but they had no option. It was Flora Day, the 8th of May, when Helston traditionally celebrates the coming of Summer. With equal reluctance Matty wore a school tie, and Jo had a head-dress in school colours. Driving into town both children cringed with self consciousness every inch of the way, but when they reached the starting point in Wendron Street they found a thousand other school children similarly dressed and all their embarrassment vanished.

"Pace yourselves," Jenny had told them, "Dancing a mile and a half is hard work!"

At ten to ten the band struck up and the dance began. The route led up and down Meneage Street, then along Church Street and Cross Street, through the gardens of Penhellis House. Then it led along Tanyard Lane, Lady Street, down to the Grylls Monument, round the bowling green, and finally up the centre of Coinagehall Street.

One, two, three, hop; one, two, three, hop! Eight bars forward, then eight bars round and round, again and again, repeated some three hundred and sixty times. It took an hour and a half to dance the mile and a half. There was a time, at Penhellis Gardens, when the dance seemed to have gone on for ever, but eventually the Guildhall was in site.

The dance over, weariness evaporated, and the children were left full of excitement. They sensed that this was something very old, and strangely important, and were pleased to have taken part.

Even so, and despite their exertions, they were pleased to get into scruffy clothes after lunch and bicycle out to Porthreun.

Matty led Jo through the bushes and out onto the west side of Porthreun. They had almost reached their lookout position when Matty stopped and turned and whispered to his sister.

"Shh!"

"What is it?"

"There's something already in the hollow."

Cautiously they drew closer.

"I think it's a body."

It was indeed the shape and size of a body. It was completely wrapped in a bundle of dark red sail cloth.

"Is it dead?"

"I don't know."

Jo tip-toed forward and lifted the edge of the sail cloth.

The bundle twitched and groaned.

"Aah!" Jo screamed and leapt backwards.

The bundle rolled left then right. Then at one end appeared a dishevelled beard, closely followed by a head.

"Mr Boscregan!"

"What are you doing here? Are you all-right?"

Mr Boscregan blinked several times.

"Jo? Matty? Oh bother. I must have fallen asleep."

"Mr Boscregan," said Jo sternly, "Have you been here all night?"

Mr Boscregan looked embarrassed.

"Yes, I have, and because you were dancing the Flora, I was on watch this morning too, but I must have fallen asleep."

Then Matty pushed forward, "You've been here every night haven't you, ever since the eggs were laid. That's why the grass was flattened."

Boscregan had now managed to unroll himself from the sail in which he was wrapped, but a sleeping bag still extended from his feet to his neck, and his head stuck out the top, like a large, whiskery chrysalis.

With his arms stuck inside the sleeping bag, he was unable to defend himself as Jo gave him a friendly kiss on the nose.

"Mr Boscregan, you are wonderful, you've been watching the nest every night and you never told us."

"I was keeping it a secret. But yes, I've been watching every night since the eggs were laid. Some nest robbers will stop at almost nothing. Jenny couldn't help because she has her rounds to do. So, I was the logical person to help."

By now Boscregan had managed to undo the drawstring at his neck and emerge from the sleeping bag. In one hand he held a telescope, in the other a thermos flask.

Matty wondered what else was hidden in the sleeping bag.

"I think morning coffee is required," said Boscregan, "Would you care to join me?"

Together they shared Mr Boscregan's coffee.

"Would you like to look through my telescope?" he said, "It's rather different to the binoculars."

That afternoon the sky was hazy, and a watery sun cast a flat light into the cove. The absence of heavy shadows made looking into the crevice easier than normal.

Matty looked again. "Yes, her behaviour is normal, but her appearance isn't! She's sitting differently. In fact, from the way she's sitting, I think the eggs might have hatched. Here, take a look."

Jo took the telescope. Branwen was sitting patiently on the nest. Bran swooped down with a beak full of breakfast. Then Branwen stood and three open mouths were visible as Bran fed them each in turn.

"Three, all three have hatched!"

Jo was right. Bran had been patiently feeding Branwen for well over two weeks as she kept the eggs warm with her soft breast feathers. For the last two days she had hardly moved, but now she shifted and stirred on the eggs as they began to hatch.

Hatching did not happen instantly. First a tiny crack appeared near the blunt end of the shell, made by the horny protrusion on the chick's upper beak called the egg tooth. For nearly a day, the crack slowly grew as the chick worked away. There were pauses while it rested, then it would continue until the egg split or there was a hole big enough for the chick to emerge.

At that moment a chick was born. It was naked and featherless, blind, and bony. The scrawny skin was home to scruffy tufts of black fluff. It was noisy, vulnerable, and beautiful.

After the first chick was born it lay still and quiet for some seconds, shocked at leaving the egg. Branwen picked up the bits of broken shell and jettisoned them over the side of the nest. As she did so the chick cried out in a mixture of surprise at being alive, and hunger. Bran was attentive and brought soft food immediately. Without down or feathers the chick still needed Branwen to keep it warm, as did the remaining eggs. Over a period of thirty-six hours all three eggs hatched.

Matty took the binoculars and a huge smile spread across his face.

"Brilliant," he said, "We've done it!"

Boscregan stroked his beard.

"Not quite," he said, "A successful hatching is indeed good news. In a few days the little egg tooth that the chicks used to break open the egg will disappear, and their beaks will look normal. Then they begin to open their eyes and small amounts of feathers start to emerge from the skin. After five days, a chick will have grown a bit and will be able to stand up and call for food.

"But the chicks are very vulnerable, and it'll be quite a while before they can fend for themselves. We must just continue to keep the whole thing secret and try and make sure the nest is undisturbed. Our job has not changed at all."

Sky-Gazing

On the next Saturday, the moment the twins arrived at Porthreun it started raining. Soon the heavens emptied.

"We'll be soaked," said Matty.

"No one would come nest robbing in this," said Jo, "Let's go to the Coastguard Hut."

Minutes later they were damply knocking on the door of the hut.

"Come inside before you get washed away," said old Billy, genial as ever. "I'll put the kettle on. I'm surprised you didn't see this coming."

Soon they were thankfully clutching hot mugs of cocoa.

"Let me explain," said the coastguard, "If you know what to look for, you can often tell what the weather's going to do.

"The first thing is to find out where the wind is coming from. Turn your head until the wind is full in your face. If you're indoors just turn your head until the clouds seem to be coming straight towards you."

"We were taught that when we learned to sail at Gillan Creek."

"Good. Well, next you just look to windward and see what's coming your way. From here on the cliff the horizon is about 20 miles away, but you can often see the weather twice as far as that."

"But you can be even cleverer if you know what to look for. You've heard of the Gulf Stream, that carries warm water from the Gulf of Mexico across the Atlantic?

North of the Gulf Stream, in the direction of the North Pole, the sea is cold and so is the air above it. South of the Gulf Stream the air is warmer. The boundary between the warm and cold air is called the Polar Front. But this boundary is not a straight line. It has curves and eddies that become the travelling weather systems that we have in Cornwall, warm and cold fronts they are called.

"So, we look out to windward. But now we look high in the sky. The first clues of an approaching weather system are wispy clouds made of ice crystals high in the sky and far to the west. Gradually they come towards us, increasing until they cover the sky.

"As the hours pass the cloud thickens and gets lower and lower. Then rain falls, softly at first, but getting harder.

"When the warm front arrives, the cloud is low, and the rain is heavy. Then as it passes the temperature rises. The rain may ease; the cloud may thin or become scattered. All will be peace for a time – but that could be minutes or hours. Then follows a cold front. From the west come towering castles of cumulo-nimbus cloud. They bring heavy rain, sometimes with sleet or hail. Fortunately, they usually pass swiftly.

"So just by using our eyes we can tell what's going to happen."

"Jenny has lots of weather sayings," said Matty.

"Such as what?" asked Old Billy.

"The higher the clouds, the finer the weather."

"Quite right, that's when a weather front is a long way away."

"Here's another. Clouds like towers, sudden showers."

"Yes, that's when a cold front is near. You see, both of those old sayings are true."

Jo suddenly interjected, "Hurrah for the old wives!"

The coastguard gave her a very strange look.

Seagull

Close under the cliffs of Porthreun the fishing boat was not visible to the coastguards. There the skipper decided to dump what was called his 'by-catch' back into the sea: fish that were above his quota, or species he was not allowed to sell. The boat was always followed by hopeful gulls, but now hundreds seemed to appear from nowhere, the sky was full of screaming, diving, hungry birds.

Then, as quickly as it had appeared, the boat continued round the Lizard and on to Newlyn. But many of the gulls remained, searching for scraps.

Bran was foraging on the cliff top, and Branwen was on the nest with her chicks when a dozen gulls swooped into Porthreun. Gulls will eat unprotected chicks, and if two or more attack a nest, then defence can be impossible.

Not two but five gulls spotted the nest. Branwen covered the chicks with her body as in turn the gulls swooped towards her. But the nest site had been well chosen. The crevice in the rock was wide enough for a chough, but too narrow for a herring gull to make a hit and run attack. The gulls dived and darted at the crevice. Their cries and flapping wings were relentless, terrifying, but they could not get close enough to strike.

Branwen thought the danger was past when the smallest gull misjudged its approach and crashed into the crevice. Bruised, but otherwise unhurt, it struggled to its feet, inches from the nest. It was bigger than Branwen and could reach further. As it jabbed at Branwen's head, she jerked from side to side to avoid the cruel strikes, but some she could not avoid without exposing the chicks. Soon she tired. The gull was relentless, more and more blows were striking Branwen. She was crying with pain and fear, only half conscious, and the gull knew it was winning. Branwen valiantly protected her chicks and did not move from the nest, but she was sure her last moments had come.

The gull paused for a second, planning a final strike. Branwen closed her eyes. Suddenly she heard a scream of surprise and pain. The gull, its wings pinioned by the walls of the crevice, was struggling to turn or to walk backwards. On its back was Bran, digging his beak into the gull's neck and head, striking again and again. Somehow the desperate gull managed to shuffle backwards and tumble out of the crevice. It managed to open its wings and soften the fall before crash landing on the rocks below. There was a moment's silence, then a chorus of seals barked loudly at the gull, and ruefully it flew out to sea.

Bran surveyed the scene. The outer edges of the nest were broken down. Branwen's feathers were bloody from several stab wounds. The chicks were unharmed and hungry as usual. First, he fed Branwen, then the chicks. Last of all he fed himself.

The Three Fortunate Bequests

This time, supper was at Clome Cottage. Megan had made Cornish pasties and brought them wrapped in tin foil. Jo had made a pineapple upside-down cake. Mr Boscregan insisted on making a mysterious sort of custard; it turned out rather lumpy but tasted very good. The meal was great fun, with jokes, anecdotes and riddles being shared by the diners.

It was Mr Boscregan that started it, "What bird can we hear at the dinner table?"

Everyone listened carefully.

"I can't hear it," said Matty.

"Nor me," said Jenny.

"A swallow."

"Oh no, that is terrible!"

"What bird is always out of breath?"

"Don't know."

"A puffin."

Groans and laughter echoed around the table.

"I've got a bird poem," said Jenny. "A funny old bird is a pelican. His beak holds more than his belly can!"

And so it went on.

Then, after the washing up was done Megan, usually rather shy, surprised everyone.

"I've got another 'three brothers' story for you. My stepmother's family came from North Wales, a place called

Cerrig-y-druidion and they had this from their friend, Lewis Evans."

There once was a poor man who had three sons: John, William, and Robert. This poor man had a cockerel and a cat and a ladder. When he made his will he left the cat to John, the cockerel to William, and the ladder to Robert. Then they all set off to find their fortunes.

Brother John put the cat on his back in a sack and travelled to a far distant land. There he found a place to lodge. But when it was bed-time the lodgers were all asking, "Whose turn is it to stay up and watch for mice tonight?"

Then John said, "There's no need for anyone to stay up all night. I have something in my sack that will catch any mice."

So, everyone got a good night's sleep. When they came downstairs, they found that John's cat had killed all the mice. But, in that country there were no cats, so they were all amazed.

"Will you sell it? How much will you take for it?" they asked.

"They're a hundred pounds in my land," he said.

So, they paid him a hundred pounds.

Then they were pleased with the cat, and he was pleased with his hundred pounds. So, he went home contented.

Brother William put the cockerel on his back in a sack and he too travelled to a distant land. He too found a place to lodge. But when it came to bed-time, the lodgers were all asking, "Whose turn is it to stay up and watch for the dawn?"

Then William said, "There's no need for anyone to stay up all night. I have something in my sack that will wake us when it is dawn."

So, everyone got a good night's sleep. At dawn the cock crowed and woke them all up. But in that country, there were no cockerels, so they were all amazed.

"Will you sell it? How much will you take for it?" they asked.

"They're a hundred pounds in my land," he said.

So, they paid him a hundred pounds.

Then they were pleased with the cockerel, and he was pleased with his hundred pounds. He too went home contented.

Brother Robert put the ladder on his back, and he too set out to a distant land. Of course, it was a land in which there were no ladders. He came to a mansion and hoping for lodgings he knocked on the door. But there was no reply, for inside there was much weeping and wailing and his knocking was unheard. He listened at the door, and it seemed that the daughter of the family was dreadfully ill, and they needed a doctor.

So, he put his ladder against the wall of this mansion, climbed it, and listened to the daughter talking in her bedroom, and he could hear that she was pining for her boy friend.

Then Robert knocked again at the front door until he was heard.

"Who are you?" they said.

"I'm a doctor," he replied.

"Please examine our daughter," they begged.

So, he popped upstairs, and pretended to examine her for five minutes. Then he came down.

"What she needs is a husband," he said, "And then she'll be fine."

"Thank you," they said, "We'll agree to her marriage straight away. What's your charge doctor?"

"A hundred pounds, please," said he.

So, they were satisfied, the daughter was very satisfied, and he was exceptionally satisfied with his hundred pounds.

Then, with all that money, the three brothers lived in contentment for the rest of their days.

Megan finished the tale with these words: "They were all happy, and so are we. Let's put the kettle on and have a cup of tea!"

There was a pause, then everyone applauded and Megan grinned. Jenny put the kettle on.

Mr Boscregan spoke. "There are many more stories about three brothers, such as the famous tale of the Three Rings in the play Nathan the Wise."

"I think I've got another one," said Megan, emboldened by her success, "It's in the Welsh epic called the Mabinogion. The sons of Llŷr are Bran and Manawydan, and Efnysien is their half-brother. So that makes three."

"Why didn't I remember that!" said Boscregan, "But wait, do half brothers count? Also, those three weren't really friends."

"So which story goes with the Three Brothers of Grugwith?" asked Matty.

"We can't tell," said Mr Boscregan. "Apart from the Mabinogion, all the tales we've discovered were published after 1748 when the Three Brothers were shown on Thomas Martyn's map. Any of those tales could be associated with the Three Brothers, and there are certainly lots more that we don't know."

Four Legs Bad

Next week, from the opposite side of the porth, Matty trained his binoculars on the nest.

"Something's happened to Branwen. She's all dishevelled. It looks as if she's been in a fight."

They both studied the nest for another ten minutes.

Jo answered, "You're right. She looks as if she's been through a hedge backwards, but I think she's OK. She's sitting up, she's alert, and Bran is feeding her normally."

Matty looked again. "Yes, her appearance isn't right, but her behaviour is normal. I hope the chicks are all well."

After a couple of hours observation, it was clear that the chicks were indeed thriving, and now their eyes were open. They no longer needed the constant warmth of their mother or endless feeding and occasionally Branwen would take the opportunity to fly to the cliff edge and feed. The chicks would call when hungry, which was often, so Branwen or Bran, never more than a few seconds away, were still busy. But at least the adults now had a little more time to feed themselves.

Through the binoculars the children could see the chicks' heads peering from the nest and sizing up the world. Every so often they would see a chick stretch out its featherless wings. Occasionally there would be a commotion as a chick decided to clamber about the nest and its siblings struggled to get out of the way.

Then from Kennack Sands away to the south-west came the sound of excited barking. A man and woman with three dogs were approaching Porthreun on the Coast Path. Two were small terriers which were running free, chasing anything that moved, be it beast, bird, or branch. Small birds fled in alarm; seagulls looked annoyed, wondering if the dogs were good to eat. Luckily there was no livestock nearby. The owners didn't seem to care.

Jo looked concerned, "Those dogs look as if they could be dangerous."

Matty added, "You're right. Rushing about like that they are a hazard to wildlife and to themselves. I've heard of dogs running straight off the cliff before now. They should be better trained, or on a long lead, or both."

"They are small enough to get through the blackthorn and gorse, and just running and barking they could frighten Branwen off the nest. Dogs like that are used as rat catchers. If one of them scrambled down the back of the crevice it could get the chicks. …"

Jo stopped speaking and watched in surprise as Matty took off running down the Coast Path towards the oncoming holiday makers. Worried at what he might do she chased after him.

"Hello," Matty cheerfully greeted the holiday-makers, "What great dogs you've got."

The holiday makers smiled, and Jo's jaw dropped.

"Are you here on holiday?"

"Yes, we're at the park beyond Kennack Sands."

Matty continued, "Did you hear, there were some rock falls in the winter. The cliffs up ahead are still dangerous. To keep your dogs safe, it might be an idea to put them on a lead for a mile or so."

"Why, thank you very much. How nice to meet such considerate youngsters. These days most people are so thoughtless."

Jo had a sudden coughing fit, but soon got over it. Then the children watched as the dogs were summoned and, with some difficulty, attached to their leads.

"Enjoy your walk," said Jo, "It's a lovely day."

"We will. Thanks for your help."

The visitors went on their way; the dogs tugging at their leashes.

"Matty," said Jo, grinning from ear to ear, "You told a lie!"

"Did I? Not really. There were rock falls in the winter, but I admit that they weren't right here. And the cliffs at Porthreun are dangerous."

"Hmm!" Jo looked unconvinced, "Exitus acta probat."

"What? What have bats got to do with it?"

"It's Latin. It means the end justifies the means."

"Is that good?"

"It is if it keeps the choughs safe!"

A Riot in the Nursery

As May drew on, the days were warmer. Sea Campions, Stonecrops and Thrift brought colour and light to the cliff face. Bird's Foot Trefoil, known as 'bacon and eggs' to the twins, gleamed the colour of the early summer sun. At the lookout Matty and Jo did not need quite as many layers of clothing to keep warm. But the ground was still damp and camping stools were needed to sit on.

It was Matty's turn to look through the binoculars first.

A smile spread across his face.

"I think there's a riot in the nursery!"

Jo was still struggling to unfold her stool, which had spontaneously turned itself inside out in a manner that no human could possibly replicate. Eventually she folded it into submission, sat down, and took the binoculars.

Matty was right. Now the chicks were not just calling for food and thrusting their open beaks towards the sky, they were scrabbling about the nest, trying to anticipate where the next morsel was coming from. The result was a wild confusion of flapping wings, heads, and feathers.

Bran and Branwen no longer flew a continuous meal delivery service; but responded to cries for food from their family.

It was clear that the chicks were now much more robust and getting stronger every day.

White Spitfires

"Mr Boscregan?"

"Do you think it's true?"

"Do I think what's true, Matty?"

Matty, Jo, Jenny, and Megan were sitting on the side benches in Can Reun, Mr Boscregan's yawl. Mr Boscregan was perched on the steps leading up into the cockpit. A candle lantern swung from a hook in the cabin roof. They had gathered for Sunday stories: Mr Boscregan's way of returning Jenny's hospitality.

"The tale about King Arthur returning to protect his people, do you think it's true?"

Mr Boscregan thoughtfully stroked his beard, "It doesn't sound likely, does it? Most people will either tell you it's a load of nonsense, or that it's something to do with heritage, imagination, and inspiration. But I do have a story about this sort of thing."

"Do you remember Jenny telling you about the radar stations on Goonhilly Downs during the Second World War? They were there to detect enemy aircraft and to direct Hurricane fighters from Predannack to intercept them.

There were airfields and radar stations all along the south coast of England. The German leader, Hitler, wanted to invade Britain, but he did not dare sail his invasion barges across the English Channel whilst the Royal Air Force controlled the skies. So, in 1940 he sent his aircraft to bomb the airfields and shoot down our planes.

Our problem was that we were hugely outnumbered. The RAF only had only 750 aircraft; the enemy had 2,500. Day after day the attacks continued. Hurricanes were sent up against the German bombers, Spitfires against the fighters. But by mid-September our pilots were exhausted. They were willing, they were valiant, but there were not enough of them. The enemy gathered for a final destructive blow and set out for England.

But at the height of the battle, when the sky was dark with enemy aircraft, our ground controllers received reports of a squadron of white Spitfires, fearlessly plunging into the thick of the battle, protecting our pilots, and driving away the enemy. No one knew where they came from; no one knew where they went. They flew out of the sun, and they returned to the sunset. But from that moment faint hearts were revived; every man and woman had new courage. The battle was fierce, but on 15 September the tide was turned, which is why that day is called Battle of Britain day.

The truth is that an invasion was prevented because a small number of very brave and skilled men overcame a much larger number of brave and skilled men. Those RAF pilots are still called 'The Few' because Sir Winston Churchill, the Prime Minister, said, "Never in the field of human conflict was so much owed by so many to so few."

"Most people say that the white Spitfire story is just a tale invented to motivate our pilots or reassure the public, or maybe they were just unpainted aircraft rushed into service straight from the factory. Others say it was just wishful thinking, a folk memory of a hero of the past. One or two romantic people say that they were flown by Arthur and his knights, returned to defend their kinsmen at their hour of need.

"But, as long as we remember to salute The Few, does the literal truth of the story matter? In 1940 the battle was won. People rightly look on the heroism of our pilots the same way as they think of the heroism of King Arthur. I think we can look at the chough legend in a similar fashion: as truth, as a story, or as folk memory. Each is valid in its own way."

Matty looked serious. "Yes, it would be wrong to take anything from the bravery of the real pilots. But it is a good story."

Can Reun gently rocked on her mooring, watched by a lone heron: a grey ghost at the water's edge.

Steps into the Unknown

Small children often have an irresistible desire to balance along the top of walls. Perhaps this is a trait inherited from birds.

There is a time, about four weeks after hatching, when a chick's increasing leg and wing strength at last matches up to its curiosity and it manages to hop onto the side of the nest. But then, ahead of it is an unknown world. There is short slope of grass then a drop of 150 feet to the sea. The sky is infinitely high. The horizon is very far away.

Once the child is perched on the wall it inevitably reaches out for a helping hand to ensure it doesn't fall. Usually, mum or dad provide the necessary stability, reassurance, and a safe mode of descent.

However, the chick is on its own. It can turn only with difficulty; it cannot yet fly. The result is much panic-filled cheeping, shuffling of feet, and undignified flapping of wings. There can only be one of three outcomes. Either the chick stays where it is, it falls back in, or it falls out.

Of course, balancing on the edge of the nest is only ever preparatory to the two remaining options. Falling back in presages climbing back up. The ultimate outcome is predictable and inevitably outwards.

This small pantomime was witnessed by Jo and Matty with a mixture of concern and amusement. Their dialogue provided a spontaneous commentary on the action.

"Oh no!"

"Come on, you can do it!"

"Don't be so silly."

"No, there isn't room for two."

"Hooray!"

"Silly bird!"

"At last."

The watchers could not know how Bran and Branwen viewed these efforts. Certainly, the adult birds enjoyed an extra moment or two of relaxation between the endless feeding and nest cleaning tasks. They could feed themselves the choicest grubs instead of giving most away. But one adult was always close by, ready to take on any predator.

Over the course of the weekend, once the first great step from the nest had been made, the inevitable follow up was getting back in, a mixture of leaping, scrabbling, slipping, and flapping. However, by Sunday afternoon all the chicks had learned the best combination of techniques and, though ungainly, could enter and leave the nest without excessive drama.

At that point the chicks' true education began. Bran and Branwen would perch on the cliff top near the nest. The chicks would scramble up after them: hopping, walking, and flapping onto level ground. On the cliff top, when they cried for food, they were sometimes fed, but at other times they were led to good feeding places so they could start to feed themselves.

Also, on the cliff top there was room for more experimental flapping. Initially this was comically ineffective. The chick's wing feathers were not fully grown, and the wing muscles were undeveloped. But over days and weeks the flapping became first single then multiple powerful strokes which could be seen to be lifting the bird's body, if only for a moment.

Their progressively increasing wing-strength gave the chicks a repertoire of movement. They could walk, hop, and run to play with their parents and siblings. Increasingly they would feed themselves, though if unable, unsuccessful, or lazy, they would call for food from their parents.

Also, the chough chicks no longer only cried out when hungry. While learning to fend for themselves they found their voices. They learned to call to parents and siblings, announcing a find of food, showing concern or fear if a parent was somehow not in sight. Within just a few weeks they became the 'chattering sea-crows' that accompanied the songs of Calypso, as she worked her loom with a golden shuttle.

Aerial Combat

Jo peered intently through the binoculars at the family of choughs on the cliff top above their nest. Though identifiably part of the family the chicks were increasingly independent. They could not yet fly, but they walked, hopped, and leapt with fluttering wings as they fed on their own. Bran looked on, half watching his family, half looking out for predators.

Matty was counting seals and writing in his notebook. When he finished, he looked inland to see what was going on. Scanning the sky, he saw something Jo could not. Circling in the thermals about half a mile inland from the cliff edge was a buzzard.

Half as big again as a chough, the buzzard was hungry. As it circled, its attention was on the ground. It was looking for small mammals, small birds, fledglings of any size. Fast and powerful, with fearsome talons and beak, it was more than capable of hunting a pigeon, a crow, or a rabbit.

The buzzard rarely came close to the coast, for the seagulls there could hold their own in a fight, and they usually outnumbered the buzzard.

But on that day a fishing boat on its way to Newlyn had tempted most of the gulls away to the south-west. The buzzard allowed itself to drift southwards to soar in the rising air above the cliff edge.

Matty spoke softly but urgently.

"Jo, Jo, look over there, it's a buzzard. Each time it circles it's getting closer. It won't be long before it sees the chicks on the ground."

"I don't think we can frighten it away. We might just frighten Bran and leave the chicks vulnerable."

But even as they were pondering what to do, the buzzard saw the family of choughs and began flying in their direction to devise a plan of attack. Bran saw the danger and called in alarm. The chicks were scattered along the cliff edge. Painfully slowly they walked, hopped, and fluttered towards him. Bran flew towards them, and on landing held his wings outstretched to make himself look as big as possible.

This had no effect on the buzzard. It was used to attacking crows, and that is what it now perceived. It selected the chick farthest from Bran and began a gentle dive towards it. Desperately the chick looked for cover; there was none, and it gave pitiful cries of fear. Bran called out and ran towards the chick, but he knew the buzzard would get there first.

Jo's heart was in her mouth as she saw the situation unfolding.

Matty just repeated, "No, oh no," again and again.

Then suddenly the buzzard looked up instead of down. Branwen had climbed unseen behind the buzzard, then with the advantage of height dived down from above. At the last instant, the buzzard heard the sound of her feathers rushing through the air. Branwen, talons extended, was about to hit the buzzard on its neck, when the buzzard folded its wings and rolled onto its back, so its own talons were pointing upwards. The buzzard dropped like a stone for several feet. Branwen missed, but not by much, and she still had the advantage of both height and speed.

The buzzard somersaulted onto its front and tried to turn towards Branwen, but she was much nimbler, and turned inside the buzzard, again positioning herself above and behind, ready for another attack.

Again, Branwen dived, again the buzzard folded its wings and rolled in defence, but again losing valuable height. For a third time Branwen repositioned for an attack, despite the buzzard's attempts to turn inside her.

Matty whispered, "I don't think the buzzard can win. Every time it defends itself it loses height, and it can never get into a position to attack Branwen. Eventually, it will be driven onto the ground, where it will be at an even bigger disadvantage."

Jo looked back at the cliff top; there was not a chough in sight. Bran had herded the chicks into the nest, and in the crevice in the cliff they were safe. Now Bran was getting airborne to join the fight. This was too much for the buzzard, which decided to trade its remaining height for speed and dived inland to its normal hunting ground. Branwen chased it for a few seconds but could not keep up. Then with a cry of triumph she turned, dived into the rising air at the cliff edge, and soared vertically above the nest.

"That," said Jo, "was terrifying but brilliant. Branwen wasn't the biggest or the fastest, but she was the most agile and she was the cleverest."

"I think," said Matty, "That although it's a smaller bird, for its size the chough has bigger wings. That's why it can manoeuvre so well."

"I hope we never have to see that again. I'm shaking."

"Me too. Let's have a cup of tea."

An hour later, back at Clome Cottage, the children's voices were still charged with energy as they described the aerial fight.

"In a way," said Jenny, "It makes us think what The Few were facing in their Hurricanes and Spitfires. They were fighting for their families and homes as well."

"I think the worst thing," said Matty, "was that we could do nothing to help at all."

Jenny nodded. "It's sometimes like that, being a nurse. You want to help all you can; you wish you had magical powers, but despite all your skills and efforts, you still finish up just being a watcher."

Traffic and Pasties

Next day, the vigil was not fun. The tail of a weather front brought a succession of blustery showers throughout the day. The choughs seemed unconcerned at the changeable weather; but despite anoraks, plastic macs, and the tarpaulin, Jo and Matty were wet and cold. At the end of the vigil, the ride back to Gweek was equally unpleasant. A gusty westerly wind had made pedalling across the exposed downs hard work. As they freewheeled down Gweek Drive the conversation was all about roaring fires, hot tea, and toast.

"I wouldn't be surprised if Jenny hasn't got the supper on already," said Matty, hopefully.

But when they reached Clome Cottage the lights were out, and the doors were locked. Wearily they put the bikes in the shed, got the spare key from under the pisky by the back door, and let themselves into a cold house. The Rayburn stove in the kitchen was nearly out, so Matty found more logs and opened the damper. Jo hunted for bread to make toast, but there was none. The kettle sat on the stove and showed no signs of boiling. The children were sitting dejectedly at the kitchen table and still wearing their anoraks when Jenny staggered through the door with the shopping.

"I'm so sorry. Even though the schools haven't broken up yet, the shops in Helston were crammed with holiday makers. Then on the way home there was a caravan that I'm sure was being towed by a professional comedian. It had a huge queue behind it. But I do have some hot pasties to get us warm inside."

Before long the Rayburn was making the kitchen warm. The kettle boiled and tea was made. Then Jenny showed the twins the trick of biting off the end of the pasty then pouring brown sauce inside.

"I used to get told off for doing that!" she said.

Defying Gravity

At dawn and dusk it is instinctive to look towards the sun. Mankind, animals, plants, all gaze at the miracles that are the coming and going of light.

However, if for a moment we were to look the other way, in the minutes before dawn we would see that the highest clouds are illuminated first. They gleam pink and red whilst we ground dwellers are still in half light. Similarly, in the minutes after dusk the high clouds are still bathed in light while we inhabit a darkening world. What greater incentive could there be to fly, to seek high places, to be at one with birds and angels?

It was only a little over six weeks after the chicks were learning to stand and walk within their nest. The next step was scrambling onto the edge of the nest and hopping from it. When they were strong enough the family would then march to the clifftop where there was room for enthusiastic flapping, initially for a few seconds, but progressively longer each day. Every week the chicks had grown bolder and stronger. Their wing feathers were now fully formed, and each day Bran and Branwen would lead the chicks further afield.

One warm Saturday morning in late June, Jo, Matty and Jenny were at Porthreun watching the choughs on the opposite cliff top. Bran had made his way onto the headland. Branwen was feeding the chicks some distance away. Then Bran called and Branwen flew the twenty feet or so to join him. At once the chicks realised the distance of their parents. With calls of concern the first chick started hopping towards its parents, flapping its wings. After a few feet it lifted into the air and flew. In turn the others walked, hopped, and made very short flights to their parents.

After another twenty minutes of feeding the adults had teasingly moved another twenty feet away. The chicks again ran, stumbled, and made short flights to join them, all the time crying out in complaint, but being rewarded with grubs on arrival.

Jo and Matty watched with delight, rapidly understanding the teaching process. They commented on every brief sortie.

The process was repeated all day, with increasing pauses for feeding as the hours progressed. By late afternoon the chicks were very clearly weary, and the family crept back to the nest with many cries of complaint.

The bicycle ride home was full of animated discussion about the chicks' first solo flights. The conversation was still in full flow when they reached Clome Cottage.

Jenny listened patiently to the twins' animated descriptions. When she was able to get a word in edgeways, she said, "Of course, this means that more of the hazards the chicks face are things that we can do very little about."

Jo looked sad, "Does that mean we haven't got a job anymore?"

"Not quite," said Jenny, "But it certainly will be changing."

Flying School

A week later the youngsters were flying more strongly. They would still ask to be fed and sometimes their parents obliged. But often as not the requests were ignored, and rather grumpily the chicks would find soft earth and feed themselves.

From the lookout Jo and Matty could see the heads of the choughs bobbing up and down as they dug for grubs and insects on the close-cropped turf of the cliff top.

"I remember, Mr Boscregan said they were called 'diggers' in Cornish."

"That's right. He said the word is 'palores', and that's now the normal Cornish word for chough."

"I think it's a very good word; it describes exactly what they do."

The family no longer remained very close together, but neither did they spread too far apart. The chicks would sometimes make experimental, perhaps even accidental flights, for no apparent reason. Occasionally a landing or a take-off would be misjudged, usually when a chick was caught out by gust of wind or an unexpected vortex. The result was usually an undignified flapping of wings and much desperate cheeping. Afterwards the bird would inevitably raise its beak in the air and strut away as if nothing untoward had happened.

The first time Matty witnessed such a landing, instinctively he laughed.

"That's very unkind," said Jo, "How would you like it if people laughed at you when you fell over? Do you remember the first time you tried roller-skating?"

"You're right," agreed Matty, "But looking at Bran and Branwen I'm not sure that they aren't laughing too."

But the young birds learned swiftly. As time progressed such excitements became fewer. Their first faltering flights were the start of a learning process that would see them agile masters and mistresses of the air.

Within a few days the chicks learned where turbulence was likely and how to cope with it.

The aerial manoeuvrability of the choughs was outstanding. They could soar, thought not as well as the gulls. But better than the gulls they could loop and roll like a fighter plane. In the turbulent air at the cliff edge, where the gulls had to use speed to ensure a safe margin of control, the choughs could manoeuvre with ease. At will, they could turn, sideslip, or cartwheel in the air with incredible agility. When the family moved from one feeding area to another it was like an unpredictable private air display.

Born in Cornwall

The postman's red van retreated down the lane. Jenny glumly clutched a piece of writing paper, slowly crushing it in her fingers.

The children looked on with concern. Jenny, usually so full of life and laughter, was downcast, almost in tears.

"What's the matter, Jenny?" asked Jo.

"I was so looking forward to this letter. It's from a girl who was at nursing college with me. She was my best friend and we've kept in touch ever since. Her family came from Coverack, and she wanted to come back to Cornwall to live. I was so looking forward to that.

"But on a nurse's pay she can't afford to buy a house here, and there are no summer rentals. She's tried and tried, but now she's given up and is going to work in Liverpool. It's sad. You'd have loved her; she's always doing exiting things like canoeing and mountaineering."

"I'm so sorry, Jenny." Jo and Matty gave their aunt a group hug.

"I'll get over it! But come on, let's get going. If you don't mind, I'll come and watch with you today; I need the company."

Together they loaded the Land-Rover.

At Porthreun the young birds had now established their own roosts in the same cliff-top crevice as their parents. However, during the day the family spent little time near the nest. The day was spent exploring and feeding, all the while honing flying skills. The birds were completely as one with their environment.

Occasional walkers came by on the Coast Path, but none seemed interested in going out onto the headland. The morning passed uneventfully.

At lunch time Matty rather nervously spoke to Jenny.

"I'm beginning to think those boys we met on the Coast Path were right. The tourists, the traffic, the holiday homes: perhaps we don't belong here at all."

"Matty, Jo, look at those birds. They are literally 'blow-ins', but of course they are welcome. So are you. A long time ago a wise person said to me, 'It's not if you're born in Cornwall, it's if Cornwall is born in you.' Judging people by their birthplace is no better than judging them by their clothes or their skin colour."

Absent Without Leave

Matty and Jo were fed up. There was not a chough in site. They had arrived in good time, set up their stools, taken out the binoculars, had a mug of tea and unpacked the sandwiches, yet there was not a chough to be seen.

"What's happened to them? Mr Boscregan would say they were AWOL."

"What's that?"

"Absent Without Leave."

"I hope they're all right."

"Me too."

"It's illegal, but I read that people sometimes put out poison for raptors?"

"What are raptors?"

"Birds of prey. Buzzards, hawks, kestrels, that sort of thing."

"Oh."

"Also, they sometimes leave rat poison in the open, which is also illegal."

There was a glum silence. Porthreun was strangely quiet.

"I wonder what's happened? I thought the problem would be protecting the nest and getting the eggs hatched. But now there seem even more hazards than before: dogs, seagulls, buzzards, poison. What else could there be?"

"Probably nothing has happened to them. I expect they're just somewhere else."

"I hope so. What shall we do? There are no birds to look at."

"Let's do a seal count. Then if there's no sign of them by lunch time we might as well go home."

The seals were duly counted. Then they were counted again. Then the sandwiches were also counted and, shortly after, eaten.

"Let's go home."

"Yes, let's."

They packed the rucksacks and with the usual difficulty wrestled the folding stools into submission. Taking one last glance across the porth they turned to go.

"Chee-ew-it, chee-ew-it, chee-ew-it."

Both children ducked as from behind them all five choughs flew directly over their heads.

To call it a formation of choughs would be a disservice to many other birds. Formations are the magnificent, symmetrical patterns in the sky, typically formed by migrating geese. They are beautiful arrowheads and echelons that enable each bird to benefit from the airflow over its companions' wings during long journeys.

However, although the choughs travelled together, the spacing and timing between them was apparently random, their flight paths were unpredictable and individual. This was no energy-saving tactic. It was instead a clever defensive ploy, making it impossible for any predator to plan an attack, let alone have a fixed aiming point.

"Hooray," cried Jo after they had passed.

"They must have been down towards Kennack Sands."

"I suppose Bran and Branwen have been teaching them the local geography."

Jo supposed correctly. The parents had been gradually leading their offspring farther afield. That way they learned the area, experienced different terrain, found different feeding sites, and strengthened their wing muscles. The chicks now usually fed themselves and only occasionally begged for food. They were practically as big as their parents.

Bran and Branwen had very nearly taught their family all they could.

Two Barrels

A week later at Porthreun there was again no sign of the choughs. Unknown to Jo and Matty the avian family had made their way almost to Black Head and were feeding between the coastguard lookout and the cliff edge. As usual, behind their panoramic windows the coastguards were watching the shipping and drinking tea.

Jo and Matty had tried walking towards Kennack Sands but there was no sign of the birds, so rather glumly they trudged back past Porthreun towards Black Head. In the distance they heard a sharp bang.

"What was that?" asked Jo.

"Probably a bird scaring machine," said Matty. "I expect it's inland where the crops are. It's the time of year when farmers like to keep flocks of birds off their fields."

As they approached Black Head, simultaneously they saw the choughs feeding on the headland, and a man with a double-barrelled shotgun climbing over a gate from the adjacent field onto the Coast Path.

"Please don't shoot here," cried Jo.

"It's alright, Miss, I know what I'm doing."

"But you mustn't shoot these birds."

"I've got a license."

"But they're protected."

"My license tells me 'zactly what I can shoot: crow, magpie, rook, jackdaw, geese, ruddy duck, pigeon and, last but not least, sacred ibis. All above-board and legal. It's to prevent damage to livestock, foodstuffs for livestock, and crops. Now, what's your problem?"

"These birds aren't any of those; they're choughs."

"Don't be daft, no choughs have been seen in Cornwall for decades. If they had been, the papers would be full of it. Anyway, I know a crow when I see one."

"But they have red legs."

"And my father's the King of Siam. Now if you don't mind, I'm going back to earning my living and ensuring your food supply."

The twins looked at each other in desperation.

"Look," said the gunman, "I've got a family to feed. I worked in the mine till it shut. I worked on a fishing boat till the quotas were cut. Now I just get fifty pence per bird. My kids are the same age as you. If I don't do my job, they go hungry."

As he was speaking, very slowly and deliberately Matty walked between the gunman and the birds at the cliff edge.

"Get out the way you little fool."

"Certainly not."

"Then I shall shoot anyway, and you'll have to take your chance."

Jo ran to join her brother. "You wouldn't dare."

"Oh wouldn't I."

The gun was raised.

There was an enormous bang. Jo screamed. Both children fell to the ground. As one the family of choughs flew towards Porthreun, crying loudly in alarm.

The gunman's jaw went slack. He lowered the gun and looked round.

Outside his hut stood Old Billy the coastguard. In his hands was a large flare pistol.

"Awful sorry," he said, "Pesky things, but we have to discharge the cartridges when they are time-expired."

"You old fool!" said the gunman, "You could have hurt someone."

Old Billy laughed, "That's rich. I don't suppose you were about to recklessly discharge your shotgun on a Public Right-of-Way, were you? Or perhaps fire at a species protected under the Wildlife and Countryside Act? Or unlawfully discharge a weapon within the bounds of a Site of Special Scientific Interest and the Cornwall Area of Natural Beauty? I reckon that my colleague and I just witnessed you breaking at least three laws in as many seconds."

"That's hogwash."

"You see that field boundary you just climbed over. Everything to seaward of that is part of the Site of Special Scientific Interest. The Cornish Coast Path itself is a public right of way. Oh, and you'd better put your safety catch on, that's another count against you."

"You don't know what you're talking about."

"Actually, I do. I used to be a navy firearms instructor, and then a Special Constable."

"You can't touch me."

"Nor would I want to; you are quite horrible!"

"Then stop wasting my time and mind your own business."

"That's fine by me, the police will be here soon enough."

"You can't fool me; you haven't got a telephone in that hut."

"You're quite right. I haven't. But I do have a very fine VHF radio. Would you like to see it? The longer I can keep you here talking, the closer the constabulary are getting. Come and see for yourself."

The gunman did not accept the coastguard's invitation, but began running in the direction of Coverack.

The twins dusted themselves down. They were both trembling with shock.

"Are you two all right?"

"Yes, thank you, but I was very scared."

"That's proves you're nearly normal! Come inside and have a cup of tea."

Inside Ed Treleaven was using the radio. The twins heard the end of the conversation: "… Yes, heading towards Coverack."

"What on earth did you fire at him?" asked Matty.

"Nothing at all. It was a blank, a training round in an old wartime flare gun, a Very Pistol it's called. Makes a lot of noise but that's all. We use them for training recruits. We can't have them firing real flares and frightening people."

At that point Matty nervously started to laugh.

"I hope you don't mind," said old Billy, "Through my friends in Coastguard HQ, I've asked your Aunt Jenny to come and fetch you in her Land-Rover. I don't want you cycling home after a nasty incident like this. Now, in the flare locker here I have …"

The twins looked on, expecting more incendiary devices to be revealed.

"… I have some chocolate biscuits."

Really a Family

Next week at Porthreun, Matty and Jo took turns to scan the horizon with the binoculars. Bran and Branwen were again on the cliff top above the nest, feeding quietly in the warm July sun, but there was no sign of the youngsters.

"I wonder where they are?"

"Do you think they might have left the area altogether?"

"I don't think so. By now they will be increasingly independent, but I think they need to be a bit older before they branch out on their own completely."

The twins occupied themselves with a seal count, and then spent some time trying to work out if it was true that every seventh wave was bigger than the six before it.

"It's another old wives' tale," declared Jo.

"But some waves are definitely bigger than others," said Matty.

"What if, in the old days, they couldn't count more than say, five, and seven just means some random number more than that?"

"But Mr Boscregan said that in the old days the kids in Mullion could all count up to twenty in Cornish."

"Well, perhaps it's like in stories then. In stories things often come in threes or sevens, like the Three Brothers of Grugith, or Snow White and the Seven Dwarves."

"What about Ali Baba and the Forty Thieves?"

"Huh!"

"Two twenties!"

"I was told that in the Bible forty days just means a very long time."

"Like the long time we've been waiting for the rest of the choughs to turn up!"

But about mid-day, just before the debate could turn into an argument, the three young choughs landed on the headland near their parents. Immediately Bran and Branwen hopped towards their children, and all the birds gave little calls of recognition.

"It's as if they were all saying they were pleased to see each other."

"And then the parents were asking what they had been up to …"

"And the children were explaining why they were late for lunch!"

"They really are a family, just like humans."

There was a moment of silence. The twins' parents seemed so far away.

Sixth Sense

Beneath a cloudless sky Bran stood on the headland near the Coastguard Hut, basking in the warmth from the great Sun-Bird. Branwen was close by. On the headland his three strong children searched for food, expertly using the rising air at the cliff edge to ferry them effortlessly from one patch of turf to another. Their skills matched his own, and they now knew the coast from Kennack Sands to Black Head as well as he did. They were increasingly independent.

Bran knew what his children did not: that they were perfectly capable of surviving on their own and would soon, quite literally, fly the nest. They still had much to learn, but Bran knew they were good at learning, and there were some lessons they would have to teach themselves. In three years, perhaps even two, they could be raising families of their own. Both he and Branwen felt a great sense of completeness. By some age-old instinct they had been called to a new land, they had met, and against all odds they had raised a family.

But at the end of the day Bran's sense of well-being vanished. Birds sense many things in common with humans, including fear, anger, and the need to protect the family. But they also sense things we cannot always detect, such as fear in others. That afternoon Bran had such a feeling. He was suddenly alert. He looked at Branwen, he looked at his offspring. They were strong, they were powerful, they were confident. He called to them.

The coastguards' shift was nearly over. The weather was good; there was nothing unusual about the coastal shipping, and the final log-book entry of the day had been written. Old Billy's gaze wandered to the little group of black birds at the cliff edge. He and Ed Treleaven were well-aware of Jo and Matty's self-imposed task of the Summer. They were pleased that the secret had been kept and the choughs were thriving. But both men were startled when the larger of the choughs gave a loud cry, unlike anything they had heard before, and the whole family took off together and flew towards Porthreun, calling again and again to the sky.

The Return of the Native

It was the first day of the Summer Holiday and the sun was shining.

At Porthreun Jo and Matty had just finished a seal count; the numbers were encouraging. The choughs were not to be seen, but this was to be expected. The young birds were now following their parents further and further afield, completing the process of learning the landscape, honing their flying skills, and finding the best places to feed. They were within days of leaving the family as fully independent, adolescent birds.

Happy that both the seal colony and the choughs were flourishing, Jo and Matty decided to return to Clome Cottage. They pushed through the bushes towards where they had left their bikes. Jo was leading, when suddenly she ran forward, crying out.

"The bikes are gone!"

Sure enough, the grass was flattened where the bicycles had been laid on the ground and tyre tracks led towards the Coast Path.

"Do you think the farmer might have taken them?"

"No, he knows us and he's friendly. But someone has certainly taken them."

"There are no holidaymakers around."

"I really don't want to walk all the way back to Gweek again."

"I suppose we could ask the farmer if we could use his phone and see if Jenny could come and get us."

"Yes, let's try that."

"And we should report to the police that our bikes have been stolen."

"I've never dialled 999 before."

"Well, I'm certainly going to do it now," said Jo.

"I wouldn't do that if I were you …"

Three figures appeared from the bushes ahead of them: Crago, Tonkin and Greaves. Crago held a crowbar; Tonkin had a large adjustable spanner; Greaves had a pickaxe handle.

"Shame about the bikes. Cheap things, they didn't float very well. But the walk will do you good. Serves you right, I say, after causing us poor, deprived local lads so much trouble.

"But there might be a chance for us to make up and be friends. We're going to see the nice people in the youth court next month. Now, if you were thinking of declining to give them a statement, I'm sure we could come to some arrangement."

Matty replied, "That would make us no better than you."

"And what's the matter with that? You're putting on your superior up-country ways aren't you, looking down on us hard-working locals. Social profiling that's called; that's very naughty. I do hope you're not going to start a fight with us helpless youths. That could get you into lots of trouble."

Crago advanced swinging the crowbar. His friends followed, barring the path. About ten yards from Jo and Matty, Crago stopped, clapped the side of his jaw, and cried out.

"Ouch, that hurt! You hit me! You nasty aggressive incomers. I shall have to defend myself against your unprovoked attack."

Matty and Jo were stunned. Never before had they encountered such calculated malice. Part of their instinct was to fight; part was to run.

"We could get really hurt here," muttered Jo, "We must dodge past them and head for the farm. If it comes to a fight, then get into a wrestling match so they can't use those weapons."

"No whispering now," said Crago, "That's very rude."

Jo and Matty ambled casually towards their antagonists.

"We don't want any trouble," said Jo, "What's it worth?"

This was not something Crago had expected. He turned to his friends. "What's it worth lads?"

Jo spoke up, "Fifty? A hundred?"

Crago turned again, "More'n that I reckon. What do you say lads? Fifty each? …"

"Now!"

At that moment Matty and Jo sprinted towards them at full speed. The lads were taken off-guard, but they were older and bigger than the twins and the path was narrow. Jo butted Tonkin in the chest, and he fell to the ground gasping for breath, but then Greaves grabbed her and held her tight. Crago tripped Matty as he ran past, and he pitched headlong to the ground.

"Now you little snitch," said Crago, "You're going to get what you deserve." He raised the crowbar above his head, ready to strike.

Jo screamed. Matty flinched and rolled aside. The blow missed.

Crago began to raise the bar again. He was about to strike when suddenly he felt a sharp pain on the back of his head. Instinctively he cried out and ducked as a large black bird swooped past him.

"Bran!" cried Matty.

"It's just a stupid bird," said Crago, "Come on lads, let's finish teaching these two a lesson."

"Crago," shouted Tonkin, "Look behind, over there."

Crago turned. Between him and the cliff edge the sky was dark, dark with black birds. There were ravens, jackdaws, rooks, magpies, and crows, and in the midst of them, five Cornish choughs, beaks gleaming the colour of blood. The great flock swooped in concert towards Crago and his friends. The boys turned to run but had hardly gone a yard when the birds were upon them. Jo and Matty watched in awe as their tormentors were driven out of sight by the army of birds, pecking, scratching, piercing.

Then as swiftly as they had appeared, both birds and boys were gone, and all was silent.

Jo and Matty looked at each other.

"Did that really happen?"

There was a flutter of wings.

"Chee-ew-it."

"Bran, Bran, thank you so much, and thanks to all your friends."

"Chee-ew-it."

Then the black bird spread its wings and rose majestically into the sky. He seemed bigger than before, more masterful.

"It was just like the story that Mr Boscregan told us." said Matty quietly, "The one about King Arthur watching out for his people."

"Perhaps it was just a murmuration."

"No, that was a conscious act by Bran and his friends."

"That was amazing."

The twins dusted themselves down.

"We'd better go, it's a long walk home."

"No, we are going straight to Porthreun farm, and we are calling the police."

They did just that. They dialled 999 and then they phoned Jenny too. The friendly farmer and his wife gave them tea and biscuits and made sure they were unhurt.

Coming through the narrow lanes from Helston the police car met three mopeds being driven wildly. The bikes turned and fled towards Falmouth at their maximum speed of thirty miles per hour, patiently followed at a distance by the police. But after only a mile the miscreants found the narrow lane was blocked by Jenny's Land-Rover. There was no escape. Loudly protesting their innocence, the three riders were taken first to Helston police station, and then to the youth custody centre in Camborne.

When the Nightjar Calls

That evening the tea-pot was again in the tree. Jenny, Matty, and Jo were sitting outside Mr Boscregan's cottage on Ponsontuel Point. Mr Boscregan and Megan had lit a celebratory bonfire, and when it was established, they took potatoes, poked lots of holes in them with a fork and smeared butter on them. Then they wrapped them in aluminium foil and buried them in the embers at the edge of the fire.

"How do we know when they're ready?" asked Matty.

"When the nightjar calls," said Mr Boscregan.

This sounded rather unlikely, but nonetheless, about forty minutes later Boscregan suddenly said, "Listen."

Sure enough, there was the 'churring' call of a nightjar sounding from the darkness.

So, the potatoes were fished out of the fire with sticks and put on plates to be eaten.

"There are too many potatoes," said Jo, "There are two left over. Whose are they?"

Jenny looked at her watch and smiled. There was the sound of an engine as a car descended the steep track to Ponsontuel Cottage. It was not a vehicle that Jo or Matty recognised.

"Who's this?" asked Matty. A man and a woman climbed out of the car.

It was Mr and Mrs Williams.

"Mum! Dad!"

The children flew to their parents' arms and there were five minutes of hugging, kissing, crying, and laughing.

Then Megan brought out some special Welsh cakes she had made, and there was hot chocolate all round.

"Just to remind me of home," she said.

"And me too," said Mr Williams.

"Lovely," said Jo, "Our Gran makes Welsh cakes too."

Firecrow

The fire had burned down but was still radiating heat. Around the embers they listened to Mr Boscregan telling stories. He had sailed all round the world in his little boat and had an endless fund of traveller's tales.

In the moonlight the Helford River gleamed silver in the darkness. Across the sky flashed a shooting star. Somewhere in the woods an owl hooted. It was a perfect evening.

"Here's one last story for you," said Mr Boscregan.

The wind had been in the east for seven days, and each of those days it got colder. At night the Moon-Bird's wings were fringed with ice, and the little Star-Birds shivered in the sky. In the day, even the golden Sun-Bird grew pale and wan. On the cliff edge the thrift gleamed with frost, the tamarisk was fringed with feathers of ice, and the earth was as hard as stone.

On the seventh day Corvus, the king of the birds, ordered the parliament of birds to meet.

"The earth is too hard to forage for grubs and ants," said Rook.

"There is no grain to steal," said Jackdaw.

"There are no acorns below the oak tree," said Jay.

"There are no scraps at the farmer's backdoor," said Magpie.

"There is nothing at all to eat," said Raven, "Even the humans are starving."

Then they all looked at Crow, for although he was smaller than many of his friends, they knew he was the wisest, so they all listened carefully.

"Without heat we will freeze before we starve. With heat we will become strong, and the earth will become soft. We need warmth. So do the humans, so do all creatures."

"Where can we get fire?" they all asked.

"From the Sun-Bird, who carries fire across the sky every day. We must get a brand from his great fire-basket and then light a fire of our own."

"Who will get the brand?" they all asked.

"I will get it, because I am the most cunning," said Crow.

They all watched as Crow flew up and up into the sky, it took him a very long time because it was so high. He knew he had to reach the Sun-Bird before it returned to its nest at the end of the day. He was exhausted with the effort, but he kept flying until he was close to the great Sun-Bird. Cunningly he approached from the east, from behind the Sun-Bird, so he could not be seen. He could see the great fire-basket on the Sun-Birds' back; he could feel its great heat. Bravely he reached out and seized a blazing brand in this beak. Then he dived towards the ground as quickly as he could.

But before long the blazing brand started to scorch his beak, turning it bright red, so he took the brand in his talons. But before long his legs too were scorched and red. The pain was great, but he knew that without warmth the birds would die, so Crow bravely held on till he reached the ground.

It took long so long to return it was dark by the time he reached the ground. But there the birds had built a great pile of twigs and branches, and dead grass and ferns. Soon it was alight, and all the birds warmed themselves, and so they all were saved.

"Well done," said Corvus, the king of the birds, "Because you brought us fire, from this day you shall have a special name, you shall be called Fire-Crow, and your family will bear that name for ever and ever."

And we can recognise that family to this day, because they all have beaks and legs that are coloured bright red. To this day it is their sacred duty to bring warmth and light to those who need it most. If you look up to the sky on clear nights, you can sometimes see a flash of light plunging downward across the sky. That is a Fire-crow bringing warmth and light and hope to those who need it.

"And he is still there, out on the cliffs at Porthreun, and we call him the Cornish Chough," ended Mr Boscregan.

"Do you think he could light a fire?"

"He already did," said Boscregan.

Mackerel Sky

"Mackerel sky, mackerel sky, never long wet, never long dry," chanted Jenny, "We had better take macs with us just in case it rains."

"Hooray for the old wives," the children chorused.

Mr and Mrs Williams looked on in amazement.

Jo and Matty encouraged their parents into Jenny's Land-Rover.

"You must see for yourselves what we have been doing."

Twenty minutes later, from the sheltered hollow they looked across Porthreun. Below them the sea reached out its fingertips to touch the horizon. Above them the sky did the same.

There is a time in the life of the heavens, when the unseen hand of God leaves the clouds rippled, like sand moulded by a receding tide. Endless ranks of white breath glide across the buttermilk sky, and the sun hides behind this moving curtain, giving it lucidity free of shadow. Against this backdrop the flight of birds has its greatest clarity.

On the clifftop the twins related everything that had happened in the last four months. Through binoculars they watched Bran, Branwen and their family. Aided by their own experience, Jo and Matty pointed out the distinctive flight of the chough to their parents. In the turbulent air of the cliff-edge, the birds twisted and turned, swooped and side-slipped, anticipating the unseen gyres, the rotors, the vortices, the breaking waves of the invisible ocean of the sky.

Just feet behind the cliff edge the wind-swept grass was short, punctuated by clumps of thrift. The vanilla scent of broom was never far away. Further back, in the hedgerow strands of tamarisk danced gracefully in the turbulent air. In the tumbling, invisible world of the air the chough and his family hovered, darted, and fluttered from feeding site to feeding site. They called and chattered to each other as they did so: informing, guiding, warning, summoning.

The human family, happily reunited, watched the aerial display. The choughs' jet-black plumage ensured that the red beaks and legs were clearly visible.

"Do you think they'll stay?" asked Mr Williams.

"I don't know," said Jenny. "It's up to them now. We've done all we can to give them a good start, and Jo and Matty have been exemplary. Whether this family stay or not, the twins could have done no more. This summer's events have proved that choughs can survive in Cornwall if we give them a little help. What we need now are more places like Porthreun, with close cropped grass for choughs to feed, and more human support and protection."

A few yards further inland, where the grass was a little longer, there the skylark nested. Leaving the earth, he climbed almost vertically, his wings moving so swiftly they were invisible. Then from the cathedral of the sky he sang: a magnificent chorus of trills, scales, and arpeggios, beautiful beyond all human understanding. As high as a thousand feet, as long as an hour, he sang the most joyful, most exultant blessing on all the humble creatures of the earth.

He sang for Bran, Branwen, and their chicks, for all those who helped them, and for all those that will help them in the future.

Return to Clome Cottage

It was some years later. Matty and Jo were growing up fast.

On a bright summer morning they sat at the kitchen table of Clome Cottage having enjoyed a late breakfast. Mugs of tea steamed in the sunlight that streamed through the open door. Jenny spoke.

"Thank you so much for coming over. Grown ups don't very often have birthday parties, and last night was just lovely. It reminded me of your adventure with the choughs. That was really special. I thought I might even write a book about it.

"Then there was the time that you met the lovely people from the Seal Sanctuary and helped save the seal. And when I was a girl, I rescued a hedgehog. They would make nice stories too. Things like that are very important."

The conversation stopped abruptly as there was a flash of shadow in the door.

"Chee-ew-it."

Bran perched on the table. He was older now. Grey feathers surrounded his beak, but his eyes were still bright, and his call was undiminished.

Through the door they could see Branwen and several other younger choughs.

"He's come back, with Branwen and their latest children.

"Dehwelans myghtern," said Matty, "The return of the king."

Jenny offered Bran the paintbrush and he drank. At once they all remembered the day after the storm when he first drank from the brush.

"I'm sure more choughs will follow," said Jenny, "But in the meantime I think it's right that we decided to keep it all a secret. It has kept Bran and his family safe. When more choughs arrive, we can tell the public."

"Perhaps his name isn't Bran. Perhaps it's Arthur."

"We may never know his true name. For now, we must keep him safe, we must keep our secret and make sure that he and his chicks flourish. But what is certain is that when all Cornwall learns that the choughs have returned, to them he will be Arthur, the spirit of the land, the celebration of the past, the hope for the future."

The Forever Nest

Above the cliffs near Black Head, the birds wheeled, screaming in some unknowable ecstasy, tumbling in the sky, silhouetted against a cloudscape that ascended for ever, edged with a gilding of sunlight.

The white wings of the gulls painted familiar, brash, careless strokes across the canvas of the sky. Closer to the ground smaller, black, birds rose and fell with a more subtle palette of movement. They were agile, deft. Their voices were quieter; they spoke rather than declaimed; they sang rather than shouted.

As the day passed and the sun descended, the birds returned to their nests. The seagulls dispersed to ledges spread over a wide area of cliff. Their nests were well-constructed bowls of twig and grass.

The smaller, black birds retired to a sheltered, south-facing cliff. Their nests were made of small sticks and lined with grass and wool, hidden in crevices in the rock.

Somehow their presence was reassuring. It was a quiet message that what had been wrong could be put right, that the past could be reclaimed in a way that served the future.

Now the sun was low in the sky and a golden pathway stretched across the ocean to the shore. It was an invitation set aside the troubled past, to face the future with confidence, whatever fate might bring.

Bran gazed over the cove. Below him seals danced in the clear water. Evening shadows gathered as the great golden Sun-Bird took its rest.

Offshore a small gaff-rigged yawl was hove-to. Its mainsail was furled, and it moved gently under just jib and mizzen sail.

The red sails glowed in the last of the sun. On board a small group of figures took in the scene.

Bran called. In answer, from the cliff there answered generations of fire-crows, their beaks and legs gleaming in the last of the sun.

Bran looked on; they would be there forever.

Chronology

The Calling	Fri 27 March 1981
The Storm	Sat 28 March
Tending the Invalid	W/E 28/29 March
A Disastrous Lack of Chocolate	Mon 30 March
We Have Made a Friend	Tues 31 Mar – Weds 1 Apr
Well Met by Moonlight	Thu 2 April
An Elegant Courtship	Fri 3 April
The Golden Bird of Day	Sat 4 April
An Unwelcome Encounter	Sat 11 April
The Vigil Begins	Sun 12 April
A Stratagem Worthy of Odysseus	Mon 13 April
The Watchers of the West	Wed 15 April
Hot Cross Buns	Fri 17 April
Easter Eggs	Sun 19 April
The Pilgrimage	Mon 20 April
Home	Sat 25 April
Accused	Sun 26 April
The Three Skilful Brothers	Sat 2 May
Flora Day	Fri 8 May
Sky-Gazing	Sat 9 May
Seagull	Sun 10 May
Four Legs Bad	Sat 16 May
A Riot in the Nursery	WE 23/24 May
White Spitfires	WE 30/31 May
Steps into the Unknown	WE 6/7 June
Buzzard	WE 13/14 June
Defying Gravity	Sat 20 June
Flying-school	WE 27/28 June
Absent Without Leave	Sat 4 July
Two Barrels	Sat 11 July
Really a Family	Sat 18 July
Crago Returns	Sat 25 July
Around the Bonfire	Sun 26 July

Reference

'Crousa Downs' was noted in 1757, [J. E. Gover, The Place Names of Cornwall (Typescript, RIC, 1948)]

Three Brothers of Grugwith is recorded on *A Map of the County of Cornwall from an actual Survey* made by Thomas Martyn, 1748. There is debate over whether it is a man-made or natural site.

'Tolmen' is Cornish, literally a hole or burrow of stone. It is found in Borlase, W., *Observations etc.,* (Oxford, W. Jackson, 1754). It also called a dolmen (Brittany), quoit (Cornwall) and cromlech (Wales).

Black Head Coastguard Hut was in use until 1987. It is now maintained by the National Trust.

The Welsh tradition bearer Lewis T. Evans (1882-1975) learned his 'Three Brothers' story from his blind uncle, Lewis Evans (c. 1857-1897), at Hafod Llan Isa, Pentre-llyn-cymer, Conwy, in about 1891-2. The Tan y Bwlch mentioned in the tale is a small farm north of Cefn Brith, Cerrig-y-druidion.

Ken and Mary Jones founded the Seal Sanctuary at Gweek in 1975. They retired in 1988, when it was bought by their long-established manager, Mike Thomas. In 2023 it is run by the Sea Life Trust.

The True Story

Choughs nested in Cornwall until 1947. An ageing pair lived near Newquay from 1960; one died in 1967 and the other in 1973. Changed farming practices probably caused the decline. Choughs feed in short-cropped grass. Cornish clifftops were once grazed by cattle, sheep, and ponies, which kept scrub and bracken at bay. But as horses and ponies fell from use and livestock was moved inland, clifftops became overgrown. Trophy hunters and egg collectors further damaged the declining population.

After 1973 choughs were sometimes seen in transit or having escaped from captivity. Hoping to tempt them to stay, the Cornwall Bird-Watching and Preservation Society (CBWPS) prepared coastal nesting locations, some on Ministry of Defence land to avoid disturbance by the public.

The National Trust bought land on the Lizard. With advice and help from the Royal Society for the Protection of Birds and Natural England, and the cooperation of tenant farmers, they began to restore the coastal habitat, introducing moorland ponies and cattle like Dexters and North Devons. Their grazing encouraged rare flowers and plants, which also need short-cropped turf.

In 2001 three choughs were sighted at Bass Point on the Lizard. Probably originating in Ireland, two of them nested. Many local volunteers and members of CBWPS guarded the nest day and night against egg thieves, and in 2002 three chicks were fledged.

Several organisations and many volunteers now form the Cornish Chough Conservation Network, which monitors and safeguards the population, which by 2023 numbered about 200. Choughs are now seen on the coasts of the Lizard, West Penwith and North Cornwall.

What to Do

If you a find a chick on the ground with no sign of its parents, and aren't sure what to do, follow this advice chart.

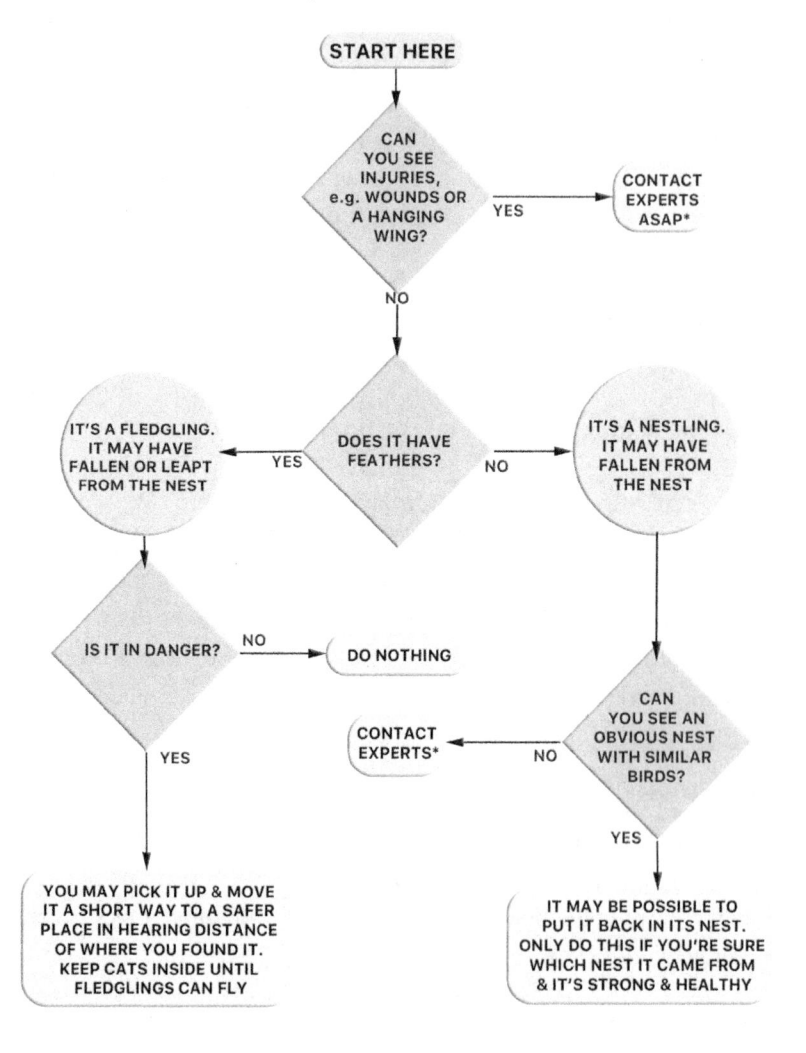

START HERE

↓

CAN YOU SEE INJURIES, e.g. WOUNDS OR A HANGING WING? — YES → **CONTACT EXPERTS ASAP***

↓ NO

DOES IT HAVE FEATHERS?

- YES → **IT'S A FLEDGLING. IT MAY HAVE FALLEN OR LEAPT FROM THE NEST**

  ↓

  IS IT IN DANGER? — NO → **DO NOTHING**

  ↓ YES

  YOU MAY PICK IT UP & MOVE IT A SHORT WAY TO A SAFER PLACE IN HEARING DISTANCE OF WHERE YOU FOUND IT. KEEP CATS INSIDE UNTIL FLEDGLINGS CAN FLY

- NO → **IT'S A NESTLING. IT MAY HAVE FALLEN FROM THE NEST**

  ↓

  CAN YOU SEE AN OBVIOUS NEST WITH SIMILAR BIRDS?

  - NO → **CONTACT EXPERTS***
  - YES → **IT MAY BE POSSIBLE TO PUT IT BACK IN ITS NEST. ONLY DO THIS IF YOU'RE SURE WHICH NEST IT CAME FROM & IT'S STRONG & HEALTHY**

*The RSPCA (England and Wales), SSPCA (Scotland), USPCA (Northern Ireland), a local rescue centre or a vet.

The Cornwall Bird-watching and Preservation Society

The Cornwall Bird-watching and Preservation Society was founded in 1931 by Lt.-Col. B. H. Ryves (1876-1961).[*] Its aims are to further the study of birds; and assist in their preservation and conservation. The Society's first project was to find the chough's remaining nesting sites and work for their safety, and the chough is the Society's emblem.

The Royal Society for the Protection of Birds

Emily Williamson founded the Society for the Protection of Birds in 1889 to fight a fashion for feathers and exotic plumes that was decimating bird populations. Her all-female society was born out of frustration that the male-only British Ornithologists Union was not acting on the issue. The Society was given a Royal Charter in 1904. Now it works in the UK and internationally in protection of birds and their habitats, education, and legislation.

Natural England

Natural England was established in 2006 to help conserve, enhance and manage the natural environment for the benefit of present and future generations, thus contributing to sustainable development.

---

[*] Invalided from the Indian Army in 1921, Col. Ryves settled at St Mawgan in Pydar and devoted his life to the study and protection of birds.

Corvids

Corvids are clever birds, often credited with personality. Most are regarded as thieves. The Jay and Magpie excepted, they have black plumage that in sunlight and close-up reveals many colours. Corvids usually mate for life. Most are territorial, social birds, often feeding in flocks. Corvids have a life expectancy of 10 years; but can live up to 20. Most are opportunistic eaters with a diet of grubs and insects, nuts, and seeds. Larger corvids will eat eggs, nestlings of other birds and small mammals. The wings of Corvids have a rectangular form with tip feathers resembling fingers.

Ravens	63 cm long 123 cm span	Up to 6 eggs	Territorial. Maintain family groups for 6 months after hatching
Carrion Crows	46 cm 99 cm	Up to 4 eggs	Often alone or in pairs.
Hooded Crows	45 cm 105 cm	3 to 6 eggs	Sociable. Only found in Scotland
Rooks	45 cm 90 cm	3 to 6 eggs	Feed in flocks. Not found in NW Scotland.
Choughs	40 cm 81 cm	3 to 5 eggs	Feed in flocks. Distinctive red bill & legs.
Jackdaws	34 cm 70 cm	Abt. 5 eggs	Noisy. Flocks roost in trees.
Magpies	45 cm 56 cm	Abt. 6 eggs	Non-breeding birds flock together. Black & white plumage, long tail.
Jays	35 cm 55 cm	4 to 5 eggs.	Shy woodland birds, fond of acorns. Pale pink plumage, black & white face & wings, white rump.

The Royal Air Force on the Lizard

Near the satellite station on Goonhilly Downs is the Dry Tree menhir, a ten-foot standing stone, supposedly resembling a tree trunk. Nearby is the burial chamber of Cruc Draenoc (thornbrake barrow). Both are late bronze age, c. 2000 B.C.

RAF Dry Tree was an adjacent World War Two radar station. Built in 1940 it had four 360 ft. steel transmitter masts and two 240 ft. timber receiver masts. At nearby Trelanvean were four receiver aerials and four transmitters. Part of the 'Chain Home' defensive network, the radars fed a Ground Controlled Intercept station at RAF Treleaver, a little further east. The Cornish radar stations were: Downderry (Seaton), Trelanvean and Dry Tree (Lizard), Sennen (Land End), and Trerew (Newquay).

RAF Predannack, near Mullion, opened in May 1941. Its aircraft included Hurricanes, Spitfires, Beaufighters, Mosquitoes, Wellingtons and Liberators. It was a base for night fighters, fighter sweeps and intruder operations over France, anti-shipping strikes, anti-submarine patrols, and defence of allied shipping during Operation Overlord. Also, it was a staging point for aircraft en-route to the North African Campaign and an emergency landing site. It was itself attacked several times.

Predannack is still a relief landing ground for Royal Naval Air Station Culdrose. A commemorative plaque at the entrance commemorates the airfield's past. It reads: "Like a breath of wind gone in a fleeting second, only the memories now remain."

About the Author

Mike O'Connor OBE is a long-time resident of St Ervan in his adopted home of Cornwall. Pilot, sailor, mountaineer, musician, oral storyteller, tradition bearer, musicologist, folklorist, songwriter, broadcaster, author - Mike is truly a renaissance man. Lauded in many fields, and well-known for his work on TV's 'Poldark', for his research and writing he has been awarded the Henwood medal of the Royal Institution of Cornwall.

Books by Mike O'Connor

Moon Over Pennycomequick In the steep woods above the Helford River in West Cornwall lives a family of hedgehogs, this is their story. A beautifully written evocation of time and place, imaginative but lifelike, heart-warming but not over-sentimental, with a light sprinkling of folklore and history. This little tale reaches out and draws you into its world, and even creates its own mythology. Ideal for the 9- to 12-year-old reader, but enjoyed by all our adult test readership.

Seal Song Seal Song is a beautiful, lyrical, engaging novella, perfect for any 12- or 13-year-old, and essential reading for anyone with an interest in storytelling, seals, or the magnificent backdrop of the Cornish coast. The tale tells of two children visit the West of Cornwall on holiday. They encounter a mysterious sailor and discover the secret of his strange voyages. But is there more to find? Of course there is; there are multiple layers of understanding to be explored. The boundaries between reality and imagination are blurred in a kaleidoscope of fact and fiction that demands to be read and then read again. It is a story of legends and folktales, myths and mysteries, loneliness and longing, kindness and love.

Cornish Folk Tales, Cornish Folk Tales for Children, Isles of Scilly Folk Tales, and **Fools and Wise Men** are beautifully crafted and impeccably researched re-tellings of traditional folk tales, all published by History Press. In them Mike draws upon his long experience as a Tradition Bearer, sailor, musician and oral storyteller.

Mike has also authored or co-authored many transcriptions and books on early music in Cornwall, also published by Lyngham House.

Printed in Great Britain
by Amazon